D1411976

CHEESE BOARDS
to share

How to create a stunning cheese
board for any occasion

THALASSA SKINNER
Photography by Erin Kunkel

RYLAND PETERS & SMALL
LONDON • NEW YORK

For Ricardo Huijon, the ying to my yang.
No matter what I do in cheese,
you are always by my side.

Art Director Leslie Harrington
Design Assistance Emily Breen
Commissioning Editor Alice Sambrook
Editorial Director Julia Charles
Production Gordana Simakovic
Publisher Cindy Richards
Food and Prop Stylist Valerie Aikman-Smith
Indexer Hilary Bird
Illustrator Cathy Brear

Published in 2019 by
Ryland Peters & Small
20–21 Jockey's Fields
London WC1R 4BW
and
341 East 116th Street
New York, NY 10029

www.rylandpeters.com

10 9 8 7 6 5 4 3

Text © Thalassa Skinner 2019
Accompaniment recipes © Valerie Aikman-Smith 2019

Design, illustration and photography
© Ryland Peters & Small 2019

ISBN: 978-1-78879-148-9

A CIP record for this book is available from the British Library.
US Library of Congress CIP data has been applied for.

Printed in China

CHEESE TERMINOLOGY

Throughout this book you'll see "PDO" and "PGI"
after some of the European cheeses and cured meats.
"Protected Designation of Origin" (PDO) and "Protected
Geographical Indication" (PGI) means that the product
is both protected and promoted by designating specific
locations, production processes and quality controls that
ensures what you are purchasing is genuine. There are
bilateral agreements between countries worldwide that accept
this, and it protects the reputation of regional foods, local
food production and its economy, and ensures top quality.

There is also an appellation system in place for most of
these foods (also used for beverages), but for the purposes
of clarity, this book uses predominantly PDO and PGI for its
protected designations. The main exceptions to this are the
cheeses of Switzerland, which are promoted and protected by
the French appellation "AOP" (Appellation d'origine protégée).
There is also France's "AOC" (Appellation d'origine contrôlée),
Italy's "DOC" (Denominazione di origine controllata),
Portugal's "DOC" (Denominação de origem controlada),
Spain's "DO" (demoninacíon de origen) and Romania's DOC
(Denumire de origine controlata).

SAFETY NOTE

Pregnant women, young children, the elderly or those with
a compromised immune system are advised not to eat
any uncooked mold-ripened soft cheeses such as brie,
camembert, chèvre or others with a similar rind. Soft
uncooked blue-veined cheeses such as Danish blue,
gorgonzola and roquefort should also be avoided.

COOK'S NOTES

- Both American (Imperial plus US cups) and British (Metric)
  measurements are included in these recipes for your
  convenience. However, it is important to work with one
  set of measurements and not alternate between the two
  within a recipe.
- Ovens should be preheated to the specified temperatures.
  We recommend using an oven thermometer. If using a
  fan-assisted oven, adjust temperatures according to the
  manufacturer's instructions.
- When a recipe calls for the zest of citrus fruit, buy unwaxed
  fruit and wash well before using. If you are only able to find
  treated fruit, scrub well in warm, soapy water before using.

Contents

Introduction

Cheese makes people smile. Simply saying "cheese" leads to a grinning photograph and instantly lifts the spirits. Delicious, satisfying and with endless flavors and varieties, cheese is often the favorite food on the table. Yet, most people actually know very little about how it is made, the different styles and how to "talk cheese". Deciding which cheese to buy is often accompanied with a shrug and eyes at half-mast. It's true that there are many, many cheeses out there. But this book will hopefully help to show you that this can be exciting rather than overwhelming.

How, then, to be confident when putting together a cheese board? Above all else, be sure to let loose and have fun. If you are not having a good time, it's likely your guests won't either. You'll find many helpful pointers here that will help to ensure your board is a hit. But the fun and personality you inject into the cheese board starts with you.

Just like anything you're not sure about, ask for assistance if you need it. If a shop has a counter or a cool cabinet filled with cheese, there will likely be at least one person around who can lend a hand. Find a board you like in this book and take in the names of the cheeses on that board. If the shop doesn't have the same cheeses, that's fine. Let them guide you to appropriate alternatives. Almost all cheeses have similar siblings that can be substituted—and that is how you learn about other cheeses. Even if you have favorites, step out of your comfort zone and try something new every now and then.

Not everyone has access to a cheesemonger, but if you do you are off to the best possible start. Dive in and befriend those folks! They'll be halving wheels and cutting cheeses daily, so there will be random samples to try, plus they will be able to open up wedges that you are interested in for sampling. The best way to learn what you like is, of course, to taste (and smell).

Most cheese counters place similar cheeses together so that you can navigate by eye when browsing. Cheese signs are incredibly helpful, and even the packaging on cheeses aims to make selection easier. A lot of effort goes into making them accurate and, often, fun. Read them carefully, learn and enjoy. Don't stress so much that you lose sight of the fact that you're choosing cheese for a happy occasion. It should be a pleasant experience, so smile, take your time and think about the end result: eating cheese!

Cheesemaking and Agriculture

Milk, the wholesome, nutritious liquid naturally produced by females after giving birth is simple in its concept but wondrous in what it achieves. What mamas eat and the state of their health impacts the quality of their milk and, therefore, the cheese produced from it. Extreme care taken by farmers in raising and milking their animals is the foundation that every cheesemaker relies on. If the milk is not excellent, the cheese cannot be either.

The main milk sources for cheesemaking are cows, goats, sheep and water buffalo. All cheeses—from fresh, rindless cheeses to mozzarella, blue and cheddar—can be made from any of these milks. The skill of the cheesemaker comes into play when reckoning with the components of each milk type and its seasonality, in order to transform the liquid into a product that can be coagulated, formed, aged, eaten and enjoyed. Not a single step can be taken lightly; when 1000 pounds of the highest quality cow's milk is to be made into 100 pounds of cheese, there is much at stake. Cheesemakers must know what they are doing and have planned exactly what they want that cheese to be before the milk warms in the vat.

Making cheese is not hard but making good cheese consistently is difficult, requiring skill, dedication and meticulous attention to detail. The basic steps to cheesemaking include coagulating (which separates the solids from the liquids), adding specific molds/yeasts, cutting the curd (aka solids), manipulating the curd in different ways (such as heating, washing, pressing, hand-ladling), then salting and aging the cheese. Every step in the recipe impacts the texture and flavor of the cheese, and every cheese produced from a single vat is different, even if it is made exactly the same way —which means it must be kept under careful watch.

The younger the cheese, the higher the moisture content and the faster it needs to be eaten. Soft cheeses with delicate rinds owe much of their texture and flavor to the rind itself, which is actively growing on the surface of the cheese and should be eaten (or else you'll be missing the point). Firmer and more aged cheeses, which cover a wide variety of styles, develop a mind-boggling spectrum of flavors due to the way that the milk's components (specifically the butterfat and proteins) break down over time and the careful treatment of the wheels as they age (whether repeatedly washed with brine or moved to lower/higher temperature or lower/higher humidity, etc.).

But nothing should mask or overpower the flavor of the milk itself—not in any cheese. No matter what, the milk is key. Remind yourself of that as you create your cheese board, making sure the cheeses get top billing and are savored. Because they are not only agricultural products but crafted with care, with millennia of practice and tradition tied to their production.

Getting Started

Now that you've decided to make a cheese board, let's talk about what this means. Either you are treating yourself, or you and a loved one (never a bad idea, especially if the weather isn't cooperating) or you've got people coming over who need feeding. The beauty of cheese boards is the ease with which they can be adjusted to accommodate one, two, 10 or 30+ people.

They can be simple and paired back with store-bought accompaniments, or much more extravagant affairs with homemade dishes served alongside. You can spend as much or as little time as you want on them, but for some people the sheer scope of this choice can be part of the problem getting started. To stop the task from becoming overwhelming, you should mentally break down the process of creating your cheese board into the three simple steps below:

1. Exploring

Musing about the flavors, finding a theme, identifying where to buy the cheeses from, choosing which guests to invite.

2. Shopping

Diving in with an open mind, a list and a purpose.

3. Serving

Putting the board together, from the base to the accompaniments and signs.

Exploring

An exciting and interesting way to think about creating your cheese board is by theme. As you browse through this book and its 25 themed boards, consider what your personal preferences are. Are you a cocktail drinker, and do you want to have some fun with cheese and cocktails? Maybe you and your friends prefer to drink beer. Or do you want to make things less focused on cheese and more about the rest of the time you have together with your friends? In that case, perhaps Less Is More would be the board of choice. Perhaps you need a cheese board to fit in around the day you are planning, in which case you might choose something like On the Go or the picnic board, depending on your needs.

Alongside your own needs, think about the other people who will be eating from your board and what might be best for them. Things to consider include:

- How many people are there?
- When will you be eating the cheese board. Before, during, after or in place of a meal?
- Do your guests have an interest in food and drink (if not specifically cheese) that you know about?
- Are there any vegetarians or people with food allergies?
- Are they friends of yours, acquaintances or new to you?
- Are there any children?

These are all things that will help you to narrow down your choices and decide amounts, types and overall selection of cheeses and accompaniments. The bottom line, though, is that you want to eat and enjoy some delicious cheese. As long as this is done, it's impossible to go wrong.

Shopping

Unless you want to pay hefty shipping fees for mail-order cheese (which will include ice packs and overnight delivery charges), you'll want to work with what is available to you nearby. The cheeses you can source locally will depend on what the stores near you can get their hands on. Start by getting acquainted with your local cheesemonger or the cheese counter at your local grocery store or delicatessen. Don't be shy about asking them for specific cheeses; they may have them stored elsewhere or perhaps aren't familiar with them yet so an introduction can lead to a wider selection for all. Another good thing to do is to go along to farmers' markets and see if there are any local small-batch cheese makers.

Throughout this book, you'll see that each cheese listed is explained with its most identifiable attributes, including at least two of the descriptive terms listed below right. Using those, you'll be able to find a similar cheese for your board. The cheeses are chosen for a reason, but you don't need to use the exact one listed in this book if you can't find it. Use the list of cheese substitutions provided or look through the cheeses available in your local shop and ponder the list of attributes to see if most of them match what you want.

If the cheese bug nabs you, there are lots of books and websites out there. Every cheese you try opens another window of discovery. Flip to the Coveted References on page 156 for a curated, cheese-centric listing.

DESCRIPTIVE TERMS FOR CHEESE
- The type of milk: is it cow's, goat's, sheep's, water buffalo's, mixed milk, etc.
- The texture: is it soft, semi-soft, hard, etc.
- The flavor: milky, buttery, nutty, sharp, stinky, etc.
- The rind (outer surface of the cheese): wrinkly, molded, hard, coated, etc.

Serving

THE TOOLKIT

You really don't need many tools to serve cheese, and it's often better to have few really useful tools than too many that will clutter up your kitchen. You'll want a sharp chef's knife (or a large offset knife) and a smaller sharp knife for everyday use with cheese. For soft cheeses, which want to stick to every surface, think thin and narrow—there are specific knives designed just for this purpose. Cheesemongers may use a single wire to make a clean cut through a soft cheese, so emulating that in a knife is the best plan.

Make sure to have a clean cutting board that is never used for slicing onions or garlic (or any other pungent food that could contaminate the flavor). If there are any leftovers, wrap them in cheese paper. It is designed specifically to let cheese breathe but not to allow too much moisture to escape, and it works well. If you can't find cheese paper, use coated butcher paper, or wax-lined paper and a plastic container.

THE BOARD

You'll want a suitable board to go under those cheeses—and there are plenty of great options out there (and probably hiding in your own cupboard, too). Size, shape, color and texture do matter here. It's better to have more room than not enough space; it's never good to have cheese, nuts, or anything else squashed up together or falling off the sides of the board. Remember to leave plenty of room for people to cut more off the cheeses and self-serve. Think about how you'd approach each cheese on the board and make it easy to reach everything you're serving. It's not fun to have to work too hard for every mouthful.

For soft cheeses, it's best to leave as self-serve. If the cheese is a small round, leave it whole but start it off with a small slice or scoop so there's no polite waiting. All rinds on soft cheeses should also be eaten; they are part of the cheese itself. Without it, the cheese would not exist. And the rind adds flavor that should at least be sampled (even if it's not your favorite part). Urge people not to just scoop out the middle.

SERVING UTENSILS

For very soft cheeses, use either a spoon or a rounded butter knife. For soft cheeses with a rind, use a knife with a sharp edge and a thin blade—there are many good ones designed for this. Firmer cheeses need a sharp edge, while hard cheeses can be "chipped" at with a small, wide blade made for this same purpose. Small tongs are very handy for picking up cut firmer cheeses, nuts, fruit and other accompaniments. Having several of these on hand is always a good idea.

SIGNS

Even if you feel that it's a bit much, don't leave out the cheese signs. Write up the name of the cheese, who made it and where, the kind of milk and rind. And add in your own personal description and thoughts on the cheese, if you want. Again, it's about having fun. Those who are enjoying your cheese board can go back and reread the signs and even snap a photo so they can get that same cheese that they loved afterward.

If you want to tell your guests more about what you're serving, opt for the choices that allow for more writing. Handwritten cards are a nice touch unless your handwriting isn't at all legible, in which case you could type them out. For the sign holders, there are lots of options out there, ranging from metal holders that literally stick into your cheese to ceramic versions that sit on top.

HOW TO CUT AND PLATE

If your cheeses are already in the sizes you want, then you're in good shape. If not, you'll need to cut them down—see the diagram on the right for a basic guide. Depending on the number of people you're serving, you may want to cut the firm cheeses all into serving-size pieces. Or you can keep a representative wedge and cut up the rest of the piece, making sure to have plenty of paste (the inside of the cheese) as well as rind on the outside of each portion. Note that if you remove the rind when cutting the cheese into portions, there is nothing to differentiate it from others on the board apart from the basic color and texture. The rind is part of the cheese—and yes, it should be eaten unless it is waxed. It is also an easy way to pick the cheese up. If the rind is waxed, cut your cheese from just inside the wax.

How to cut and serve cheese

Block

Square

Large round

Small round

Half-moon wedge

Blue vein/semi-soft wedge

Semi-hard wedge

Cylinder/log

Pyramid/cone

Fresh cheese (serve
in a bowl)

Scoop-able cheese
(break through or cut
off top rind)

Hard cheese (chip into
bite-size chunks)

Accompaniments

BREAD OR CRACKERS?

When in doubt, serve both. Some people are bread eaters, others love crackers; it's never cut and dry. When choosing, err on the side of the mildly flavored bread or cracker, since the cheese should be the center of attention. Heartier choices, like multigrain, dark and rye breads, work for the stronger cheeses, but all cheeses pair well with a fresh baguette and water crackers.

DRINK UP

A vital ingredient in cheese is salt, and it does more than enhance flavor. It acts as a preservative by controlling moisture as well as microbial activity, which have crucial affects on the aging of cheese. Salt = thirst, so make sure to have drinking water poured and ready, even if you're serving other non-alcoholic beverages—but especially if you're serving alcohol alongside your cheese. Generally, cheese and wine is many people's go-to combination, but pairing beverages of all kinds with cheese is both fun and eye-opening.

JAMS, CHUTNEYS, PICKLES & PASTES

Many wonderful fruit- and vegetable-based accompaniments load store shelves, some of which you might not even have thought about serving with cheese. Today's jam and chutney producers have unleashed their creativity, putting together fruits, herbs, nuts and spices to create fantastic condiments. They add color, texture, moisture and a palette of flavors that can raise a cheese board from good to extraordinary. Or, of course, you can choose from the tempting recipes included in this book and make your own.

FRUIT-LADEN

Fresh fruit with cheese is classic and always a good pairing, providing vibrant color on your board, cleansing the palate and counterbalancing the butterfat (especially if the fruit is higher in acid). Don't forget about dried fruits, too. These should be a staple in everyone's cupboards as they keep so well and are great for a last-minute cheese feast because their sweetness goes perfectly with almost every cheese style.

GOING NUTS

Nuts of all kinds pair well with cheese, providing textural contrast and a complementary flavour (saying a cheese tastes "nutty" is one of the most commonly used descriptors). Each type of nut, however, has a unique flavour which changes again whether roasted or raw. Both have their place on a cheese board, but pair according to similar flavors: milder, milkier raw nuts go well with creamier cheeses, and roasted nuts go nicely with more aged cheeses. You can also throw candied or flavored nuts into the mix— just don't overpower the cheese whatever you do, and be judicious about using salted nuts (since most cheese is already fairly salty).

SWEET THINGS

Honey, chocolate, caramel, shortbread, toffee, even cocoa-coated espresso beans can startle the palate and make for a superb cheese board addition. Sweet things and cheese are a good union, especially when the cheese is fairly salty. The possibilities are endless. Each of these things has its own litany of flavors and textures, so there is a wide spectrum of fun to be had.

GET CREATIVE

Placing leaves beneath cheeses adds a natural element that is both attractive and makes clean-up a snap. Fresh grapevine leaves are a classic, but some large tree leaves (sycamore, chestnut and maple, for example) are also good. Edible flowers, too, add eye-popping color and can be easily tucked into open spaces on the board or directly onto fresh cheeses. Just make sure that any leaves or flowers you use are cleaned before use, are food-safe and pesticide-free.

Bold &
Beautiful

Bold & Beautiful

Cheeses with attitude

This board is simple in its purpose while still being unusual, and it can be an eye-opener for those who don't think of cheese as having flavor extremes. Think of it as a learning tool and a means of exploration—and serve it to those who are interested in food in a deeper way. Invite your guests to taste methodically and encourage them to think about ways to describe what they taste, which is something cheesemongers grapple with daily. What is "sharp" to one person might be called "salty" or "strong" by another, so this board—which includes stellar examples of sharp, strong, stinky, and spicy—helps us to define what's what. Label the flavor descriptions on one side of the cheeses sign, then write the name, maker and provenance on the other.

Cheese Descriptions:

OMA (A)
Von Trapp Farmstead/Cellars at Jasper Hill (Waitsfield/ Greensboro, Vermont, USA)
This "stinky" cow's milk cheese is what your guests will smell upon arrival—and it's a good thing! Known as a "washed rind", its red-orange surface is the culprit. It's loaded with much-desired bacteria that thrive with moisture and omit a striking signature odor. Meat, hints of wet basement, umami—it's all there. You'll note, though, that the rind holds almost all of the pungency; the inside paste is soft, delicate and mild.
Substitutions: Grayson (Meadow Creek Dairy; Galax, Virginia, USA), Stinking Bishop (Charles Martell & Son; Gloucester, England), Taleggio PDO (multiple producers; Lombardy, Italy), Limburger (Chalet Cheese Co-op; Monroe, Wisconsin, USA), Baronet (The Old Cheese Room; Wiltshire, England).

QUESO DE VALDEÓN PGI (B)
La Caseria (Castilla y León, Spain)
This blue cheese, made from a blend of cow's and goat's

milk, has a "strong" punch that makes people sit up and take note. It's peppery (though not overly so) with plenty of bluing from the mold that turns blue-green when exposed to oxygen. The outside is wrapped in sycamore leaves and aged for over 60 days. In cheesemonger speak, "strong" is not the same as "sharp"; normally, a "strong" cheese needs an additional descriptor to place it in context, like "blue" or "washed rind". Think of a "strong" cheese as one you wouldn't have anything else to eat after.
Substitutions: Cabrales (multiple producers; Asturias, Spain), Gorgonzola Piccante PDO (multiple producers; Lombardy, Italy), Original Blue (Point Reyes Farmstead Cheese Co.; Tomales Bay, California, USA), Dorset Blue Vinney (Woodbridge Farm; Dorset, England).

PROVOLONE MANDARONE (C)
Luigi Guffanti Formaggi (Piedmont, Italy)
When thinking of "sharp" cheeses, most reach for cheddar. But this extra-aged cow's milk provolone takes it one step further, providing a lip-smacking pucker. Although you might be expecting salt, it's really a wallop

of acid that provides the sharp bite. Made by dousing fresh curds in hot water and then stretching them (similar to mozzarella), provolone has a stringy texture that becomes more cohesive as it ages. Extra aging (over 12 months) for this particular provolone makes it extra sharp. *Substitutions:* Provolone Piccante (multiple producers; Italy), Caciocavallo Podolico (multiple producers; Campagna, Italy), Seriously Sharp Cheddar Cheese (Cabot Creamery; Waitsfield, Vermont, USA), Extra Sharp White Cheddar (Tillamook; Oregon, USA), 1833 Vintage Reserve Cheddar (Barber's; Somerset, England).

BIG ED'S GOUDA WITH SERRANO PEPPERS (D)
Saxon Creamery (Cleveland, Wisconsin, USA)
The "spicy" notes in cheese can happen naturally (like in the peppery quality of Valdeón) but to really hammer it home, cheesemakers can add chili peppers. Case in point: Big Ed's Gouda, a semi-firm cow's milk cheese with a springy bite and Serrano peppers added to the paste. Due to its buttery flavor and softer texture, this peppered cheese isn't as spicy as others—but the subtle heat builds; and is definitely present. If very potent heat is what you're after, look for similar cheeses made with ghost peppers or habañero. There are varying levels of intensity and some really sear, so be forewarned. This selection ensures that nothing else on the plate will be overpowered; the fat in cheese helps flavors to linger on the palate, spice included. (Though a beer alongside helps to soothe.) *Substitutions:* Dragon's Breath Cheddar Cheese (Henning's Wisconsin Cheese; Keil, Wisconsin, USA), Ghost Pepper Colby Jack (Kindred Creamery; Wisconsin, USA), Angel de la Muerte (Cesar's Cheese; Sheboygan Falls, Wisconsin, USA), Red Devil (Snowdonia Cheese Company; Denbighshire, Wales), Teifi Sweet Pepper (Caws Teifi; Ceredigion, Wales).

Suggested Accompaniments

TO BUY IN:

dried dates
candied orange slices
thirst-quenching beer
chocolate biscotti drizzled with melted bittersweet/dark chocolate

TO MAKE:

Corsican fried olives

With their satisfying crunchy coating, these olives match nicely with a bold cheese board selection.

4 oz./115 g goat's cheese, room temperature
1 teaspoon herbes de Provence
finely grated zest of 1 orange
1 egg
1 tablespoon all-purpose/plain flour
1 cup/60 g panko or coarse breadcrumbs
40 large green and black olives, pitted
2 cups/475 ml vegetable oil
fleur de sel, to sprinkle
pastry/piping bag with a small tip/nozzle
deep-frying thermometer

MAKES 40

CHEESE LIST:

A Oma

B Queso de Valdeón PGI

C Provolone Mandarone

D Big Ed's Gouda with Serrano Peppers

Mix together the goat's cheese, herbs and orange zest until smooth. Put the mixture in the pastry/piping bag and set aside.

Lightly beat the egg in a small bowl and set aside. Put the flour on a small plate and the breadcrumbs on another.

Using the pastry/piping bag, pipe each olive full with the cheese mixture. Dip each olive in the flour, then the egg, and toss in the breadcrumbs until well coated.

Heat the oil in a heavy-bottomed pan until it reaches 350°F (180°C). Alternatively, test the oil by dropping in a cube of bread. It should turn golden in about 20 seconds.

Deep-fry the prepared olives in batches until crispy and golden brown, about 1 minute. Drain on paper towels, sprinkle generously with fleur de sel and serve.

Menagerie

Menagerie

Four different milks

When digging into a cheese platter, most people don't give a thought to the animal behind the milk that the cheese is made from. But that lactating mammal is where it all begins, and the environment where it is raised, the food it eats, the time of year the milk is produced—all of that makes a difference to the final product. This board celebrates the animal and places it front-and-center by using five cheeses, each made from a different species' milk (and one that's a mixture of several). Though it's obviously possible to enjoy cheese and never think about the source of its main ingredient, it makes sense to honor the hard-working mums whose life-bearing skills create something so complex. For fun, draw the shape of the animal on the sign above the name and provenance. Alternatively, leave signs off entirely until guests have guessed what type of milk each cheese is made from.

Cheese Descriptions:

L'AMUSE BRABANDER GOAT GOUDA (A)
Fromagerie L'Amuse (IJmuiden & Amsterdam, Holland)
Gouda made from goat's milk is an eye-opener. Aged goudas of all ilks boast a lingering sweetness that makes them user-friendly, but a goat's milk version takes it even further. Aged for six months or more in a particularly warm and humid cave, this 20 lb./9 kg. wheel is dense in body and rich in bright, caramelly flavors that belie any hint that it's made from goat's milk. But it is!
Substitutions: Honey Bee Goat (Cheeseland; Holland), Midnight Moon (Cypress Grove; California, USA), Premium Goat (Beemster Cheese; Holland), Killeen Goat Gouda (Killeen Farmhouse Cheese; Galway, Ireland), Superior Goat (Ribblesdale Cheese; Yorkshire, England).

BREBIROUSSE D'ARGENTAL (B)
Fromagerie Guilloteau (Pélussin, France)
"Pecorino" means sheep in Italian, and there are numerous pecorino cheeses made in that Mediterranean country, particularly in Sardinia. But most are firm; often they're table cheeses, used for grating, shaving and cooking. Besides ricotta, soft sheep's milk cheeses are rare. But sheep's milk is higher in butterfat and thus holds the potential to produce luscious soft wheels, like this one. Its maker, a French *laiterie* near the city of Lyon, uses a special technique to ensure the paste is extra-velvety.
Substitutions: Kinderhook Creek (Old Chatham Sheepherding Company; Old Chatham, New York, USA), Bossa (Green Dirt Farm; Weston, Missouri, USA), Wigmore (Village Maid Dairy; Berkshire, England), Flower Marie (Golden Cross Cheese Co.; Sussex, England).

CHÄLLERHOCKER (C)
Käserei Tufertschwil (Tufertschwil, St. Gallen, Switzerland)
Swiss cheeses are predominantly made from cow's milk, and exquisitely so. Gruyère, Emmentaler, Appenzeller, Raclette (all PDO)—these traditional cheeses provide a

strong backbone to the mountainous country's farming economy and traditional lifestyle. In recent years, several Swiss cheesemakers have been experimenting, making Alpine styles with unique twists. This is a great example; made by a revered producer of Appenzeller PDO cheese but aged for a bit longer than that classic. It's got a fudgy texture and flavors of roasted peanuts and brown butter.

Substitutions: Der Scharfe Maxx (Käserei Studer; Thurgau, Switzerland), Oka Frère Alphonse (Agropur; Quebec, Canada), Hornbacher (Michael Spycher; Fritzenhaus, Switzerland), Stärnächäs (Walo von Mühlenen; Fribourg, Switzerland), Le Migneron de Charlevoix (Laiterie Charlevoix; Baie-Ste-Paul, Quebec, Canada).

BLU DI BUFALA (D)
Caseificio Quattro Portoni (Lombardy, Italy).

When it comes to water buffalo, it's all about the butterfat—that's what makes buffalo milk mozzarella (a.k.a. *mozzarella di bufala*) so luscious. It's also what makes everything from Quattro Portoni—a cheesemaker with its own herd of roughly 1000 buffalo in northern Italy—so compelling. Made into a 9 lb./4 kg. square, this blue cheese is tangy but not overpowering, and the texture is crumbly yet ultra-creamy on the palate.

Substitutions: Quadrello di Bufala/Casatica di Bufala (Caseificio Quattro Portoni; Lombardy, Italy), Baffalo Blu (Caseificio Defendi; Lombardy, Italy), Pendragon Buffalo Cheese (Somerset Cheese Company; Somerset, England), Shipston Blue (Carron Lodge; Lancashire, England), Mozzarella di Bwufala Campana PDO (multiple producers; Italy).

ROBIOLA TRE LATTI (E)
Luigi Guffanti Formaggi (Arona, Piedmont, Italy)

Mixed-milk cheeses may sound unusual, but they actually make perfect historic sense. As seasons changed and milk from different herds tended to dry up, cheesemakers typically continued with whatever milk was on hand. Cow, goat and sheep are the *tre* (three) *latti* (milks) in this soft, creamy pillow of cheese, cared for by the renowned affineur Luigi Guffanti. If you close your eyes and think about it, you might taste each milk in turn: cream, butter, tang.

Substitutions: Toma Della Rocca (Caseificio dell'Alta Langa; Lombardy, Italy), Hummingbird (The Farm at Doe Run; Coatesville, Pennsylvania, USA), Cremet (Sharpham Dairy; Devon, England), Robiola Bosina (Caseificio dell'Alta Langa; Piedmont, Italy).

CHEESE LIST:
A Brabander

B Brebirousse d'Argental

C Chällerhocker

D Blu di Bufala

E Robiola Tre Latti

Suggested Accompaniments

TO BUY IN:

dry white wine
fresh baguettes
seeded crackers
roasted, unsalted cashews
fresh lemon slices and rosemary, to garnish

TO MAKE:

Candied almonds

These moreish nuts are very slightly spicy and sweet with brown sugar and maple syrup, a great foil for the savoriness of blue cheese especially.

2 cups/270 g raw almonds, skin on
½ cup/100 g dark brown sugar
¼ cup/60 g maple syrup
1 teaspoon chipotle powder

MAKES 2 CUPS/300 G

Preheat the oven to 375°F (190°C) Gas 5.

Mix all the ingredients except for the sel gris together in a bowl until the almonds are well coated. Spread the almonds on a non-stick baking sheet and bake in the preheated oven for 5–8 minutes. The sugars will bubble and turn a darker color.

Remove the almonds from the oven and stir with a wooden spoon. Set aside to cool on the baking sheet. As they cool, the sugars will begin to harden. When the almonds have cooled, serve them in a bowl with your cheese board. The nuts can be stored in an airtight container for up to a week at room temperature.

Less is More

Less is More

One cheese, single focus

Why make your life harder than it needs to be? And why not let one glorious cheese take center stage? This singular approach to a cheese board has great merit, especially when the central focus is versatile. Although it can sit out before, during and after a meal for multi-purpose grazing, this board shines when brought out after the main course to promote lingering and leisurely sipping on a variety of beverages. Let your guests self-serve and offer a variety of accompaniments to mix and match with the cheese, including chocolate and fruits (there's no need for a dessert). The simplicity makes an elegant statement yet sparks creativity—without the fuss.

Cheese Description:

AVONLEA CLOTHBOUND CHEDDAR
Cows Creamery (Prince Edward Island, Canada)
This Canadian cheddar is made from unpasteurized cow's milk and aged for over 12 months. Wrapped* in cheesecloth/muslin after production, the drum-shaped wheel then rests in a protected facility in open air, slowly losing moisture and gaining robust flavor. But it's not just acid that builds the flavor in this cheese—it is layers of complex flavors that form as the components of the milk break down. As a result, you won't just be hit by a wave of sharpness; instead you'll find notes of fresh grass, straw and butter. The texture is firm, toothsome and able to be "chipped" at quite easily with a small, wide knife. This cheese will enhance many wines rather than fight with tannins and will marry well with most beers and ciders.
Substitutions: Flory's Truckle (Milton Creamery; Milton, Iowa, USA), Montgomery's Cheddar (Manor Farm; Somerset, England), Westcombe Cheddar (Westcombe Dairy; Somerset, England), Clothbound Cheddar (Grafton Village Cheese; Grafton, Vermont, USA), Bandaged Cheddar (Bleu Mont Dairy; Blue Mounds, Wisconsin, USA).

*TIP: When serving clothbound cheddar, make sure to remove the cloth itself. It will leave its imprint on the rind, which looks rustic and eye-catching, and your cheese can be eaten completely this way.

Suggested Accompaniments

TO BUY IN:

crusty baguettes
bittersweet/dark chocolate
fresh fruits such as pineapple, figs or cherries

TO MAKE:

Nectarine & serrano paste

This sweet and spicy pairing is just sublime with cheddar. If you have a lower tolerance for spice, and depending on how hot the serranos are, then simply decrease the quantity used here. Don't leave them out as they give a wonderful kick to the sweet nectarines.

16 ripe nectarines, pits/stones removed and cut into quarters
2 serrano peppers, thinly sliced with seeds included
4½ cups/900 g granulated/caster sugar
freshly squeezed juice of 1 lemon
sterilized glass jars with airtight lids

MAKES 4 CUPS (32 FL OZ.)/950 ML

Place the nectarine quarters in a preserving pan or large saucepan and add 1 cup/235 ml of water. Bring to the boil over a medium-high heat. Reduce the heat and simmer for about 20 minutes, stirring occasionally, until the nectarines are soft and broken down.

Place the nectarines in a blender and purée. Return the purée to the pan and add the serrano peppers, sugar and lemon juice. Bring to the boil, then reduce the heat and simmer for 45 minutes, stirring frequently.

Spoon the paste into sterilized glass jars, leaving a ¼-inch/5-mm gap from the top. Carefully tap them on the counter top to get rid of air pockets. Wipe the jars clean and screw on the lids, then leave to cool. Store in the refrigerator and eat within 1 month.

CLOTHBOUND CHEDDAR

Cheddar comes in many shapes and sizes, with significant variations in taste and texture. One key divergence is "block" or "brick" cheddar versus "clothbound" or "bandage-wrapped" cheddar. Block cheddar is just what it sounds: cheddar made into a 40-lb/18-kg (or sometimes much larger) block that is then cut down into smaller blocks for wholesale and retail. These are aged in plastic, which keeps in moisture and slows down aging. Clothbound cheddar is also what it sounds: wrapped in muslin, rubbed with butter or lard and aged in a cooler/ cave. These are usually made into drum-shaped wheels called "truckles". The difference? Texturally and flavor-wise, these are not the same cheese. Block cheddars are softer, more cohesive and their flavors cleaner, often sharper. Clothbound cheddars are drier and more crumbly, with tantalizing layers of aromas and flavors.

Young & Wise

Young & Wise

Kids like good cheese, too

Never underestimate the palate of a budding adult—and definitely don't curb it. Cheese is user-friendly; it has no legal age minimum and it's a great way to draw both good eaters and less-than-good eaters into the wonderful world of flavor. The cheeses on this plate don't push too hard, but the three main milk sources (cow, goat and sheep) are represented, and each one's texture is different. To make this one elegant enough for connoisseurs, serve sparkling fruit juices alongside. You might also toss a few adults into the mix—but only if they are ready to pay attention.

Cheese Descriptions:

LAMB CHOPPER (A)
Cypress Grove (Arcata, California, USA)
Velvety and luscious, this sheep's milk gouda is made in Holland according to an original recipe from Northern California-based Cypress Grove. Its name—and label depicting a sunglasses-wearing ewe on a motorcycle—makes it lovable at first glance; for those who aren't familiar with sheep's milk in any capacity, this is a great way to get hooked. Remove the waxed rind to make serving easier. Use leftovers for grilled cheese sandwiches.
Substitutions: Ewephoria (Cheeseland; Holland), Grand Ewe (Uniekaas; Holland); Ewenique (Central Coast Creamery; Paso Robles, California, USA), Sheep Rustler (White Lake Cheese; Somerset, England).

CREMONT (B)
Vermont Creamery (Websterville, Vermont, USA)
This soft, spreadable cheese is made from a mixture of cow's and goat's milks. Its name is an abbreviation for "Cream of Vermont", and that's precisely what it is. A mild, milky flavor and silky texture are the result of a boost of butterfat from added cream, making this one a "double cream" cheese that's easy to love. Make sure that every part of this cheese is devoured, from the thin, white, wrinkled rind to its gooey paste.
Substitutions: Kunik (Nettle Meadow; New York, USA), St. Jude (White Wood Dairy; Suffolk, England), Chaource PDO (multiple producers; Champagne-Ardenne, France).

GARROTXA (C)
Sant Gil d'Albió (Catalonia, Spain)
Hard to pronounce (say "gah-roh-cha") and boasting a curiously gray rind and bright white paste, this one is the dark horse of the board. But skeptical eaters, once wooed by Lamb Chopper and Cremont, will have trust instilled—so you'll be able to convince them. When nibbled, the clean, lightly earthy and herbal flavors will win them over. Just like that, the trifecta of milks is kid-approved.
Substitutions: Queso de Mano (Haystack Mountain; Longmont, Colorado, USA), Tomme de Chèvre (multiple producers; Savoie, France), Patacabra (Quesos la Pardina; Zaragoza, Spain), Ticklemore (Sharpham Dairy; Devon, England).

*TIP: After trying each cheese and getting feedback from the kids, add the signs to uncover the milk types.

CHEESE LIST:

A Lamb Chopper

B Cremont

C Garrotxa

Suggested Accompaniments

TO BUY IN:

fresh apples

dried apricots

dried cranberries

fruit and nut biscotti

sparkling fruit juices

TO MAKE:

Extra-long Hawaiian black salted breadsticks

Children and adults alike love breadsticks, and they will go with virtually any cheese. They are especially nice for smothering in soft gooey cheese, such as the Cremont on this board. The Hawaiian black salt adds a sophisticated touch.

3½ cups/460 g all-purpose/plain flour, plus extra for dusting the work surface

1⅓ cups/325 ml warm water

3 tablespoons olive oil, plus extra for brushing

1 tablespoon milk

3 teaspoons fast-action dried yeast

½ teaspoon brown sugar

1 tablespoon Hawaiian black lava sea salt

MAKES ABOUT 24

To make the dough, put the flour in a food processor and set aside for a moment. In a glass measuring pitcher/jug, mix together the warm water with the 3 tablespoons of olive oil, the milk, yeast and brown sugar. Turn on the food processor and with the motor running, add the liquid to the flour in a steady stream. Process until all the liquid is incorporated and the dough forms a ball, about 3 minutes. Transfer the dough to a lightly floured work surface and knead for about 3 minutes. Form into a ball and transfer to an oiled bowl. Cover with a paper towel and let prove in a warm place until doubled in size.

Preheat the oven to 425°F (220°C) Gas 7.

Turn the dough out onto a floured surface. Roll into a rectangle of 15 x 10 inches/38 x 25 cm, and ¼-inch/5-mm thick. Use a sharp knife to cut ½-inch/1-cm strips of dough from the long side of the rectangle. Fold the strips in half and with the palms of your hands roll the dough into breadsticks roughly 10-inches/25-cm long.

Arrange the breadsticks over two non-stick baking sheets. Brush with olive oil and sprinkle with the Hawaiian black lava sea salt. Bake in the preheated oven for 10 minutes, turn the sticks over, and bake for another 10 minutes until golden. Leave to cool on a wire rack.

It's a Party!

It's a Party!

Celebrate with cheese

Serve bubbles alongside cheeses that love them, and you'll have reason to celebrate. Champagne and cheese is classic but not passé. The cheeses will be adored but it's the wine that really sets the tone. Steer clear of yeasty Champagnes and sparkling wines and opt for those with well-balanced crisp acidity. Ahead of your party, taste and select wedges that are just right with crisp, clean bubbles. The idea here is to lay this board out and let people self-serve over a long period of time, with plenty of good music and laughter. Pop the corks* and pour the stars; every palate will be happy and dancing on the ceiling. *Be careful how you do this—hand over cork throughout, preferably with a hand towel over it. Practice makes perfect!

Cheese Descriptions:

SAINT ANDRÉ (A)
CF&R (Normandy, France)

This silky triple-cream round has a bright white, edible rind and a buttery paste. If you're hosting a larger group, make sure to have several of these in your fridge so that when one is inevitably demolished, another is on hand. The richness of this cow's milk cheese holds a deserved place in the "go to" list for all bubbly wines, creating a perfect counterbalance. It's a crowd-pleaser for all.

Substitutions: Brillat-Savarin (multiple producers; Burgundy, France), Pierre Robert (Fromagerie Rouzaire; Tournan-en-Brie, Île-de-France, France), Délice de Bourgogne (Fromagerie Lincet; Saligny, Bourgogne-Franche-Comté, France), Finn (Neal's Yard Creamery; Herefordshire, England), Elmhirst (Sharpham Dairy, Devon, England), LaLiberté (Fromagerie du Presbytère; Centre-du-Quebec, Canada).

MOLITERNO AL TARTUFO (B)
Central Formaggi (Sardinia, Italy)

Hailing from the Mediterranean island that boasts 1.5 million people and 4 million sheep, this six-month-old sheep's milk cheese becomes toothsome and piquant before it's injected with a glorious paste of black summer truffles and extra virgin olive oil. Truffle fans rejoice: this is the best of the best. Serve a hefty wedge paired with crisp bubbly, and there's no way to deny the celebration both in the mouth and the soul.

Substitutions: Sottocenere al Tartufo (multiple producers; Veneto, Italy), Melkbus 149 Truffle (Uniekaas; Holland), Crutin (Beppino Occelli; Piedmont, Italy).

PARMIGIANO REGGIANO PDO (C)
Multiple producers (Emilia-Romagna, Italy)

When serving this classic as a table cheese, make sure the wedge is freshly cut from its 80 lb./37 kg wheel, and allow guests to chip away at the jagged interior paste. These great drums of cow's milk cheese are not all the same; some are carefully aged for 24-plus months, boasting crags and crystals, while others are younger and milder, best for grating or shredding. Small chunks of excellent "grana" cheeses are perfect with sparkling wines; the multi-layered flavors in the cheese meld beautifully with the crisp bubbles.

Substitutions: Grana Padano PDO (multiple producers; Italy), Gran Kinara (Fattore Fiadino; Piedmont, Italy), American Grana (BelGioioso Cheese; Denmark, Wisconsin, USA), Old Winchester (Lyburn Cheese; Wiltshire, England), SarVecchio Parmesan (Sartori Cheese; Wisconsin, USA), Västerbottensost (Norrmejerier; Västerbotten, Sweden), Gran Moravia (Brazzale; Moravia, Czech Republic).

CHEESE LIST:
A Saint André

B Moliterno al Tartufo

C Parmigiano Reggiano PDO

Suggested Accompaniments

TO BUY IN:

crisp Champagne or sparkling wine
fresh pears
seedless white grapes
buttery crackers
bay leaves, to garnish

TO MAKE:

Plum & bay paste

The dark ruby color of this paste contrasts beautifully with the pale, creamy cheese on your board. Bay leaves add a rich, herbal flavor to the sweet plums.

24 ripe plums, cut in half, pits/stones removed
2 fresh bay leaves
2 tablespoons Madeira wine
4½ cups/900 g granulated/caster sugar
freshly squeezed juice of 1 lemon
sterilized glass jars with airtight lids

MAKES 4 CUPS (32 FL OZ.)/950 ML

Place the plums in a large saucepan and add 1 cup/ 235 ml of water and the bay leaves. Bring to the boil over a medium-high heat. Reduce the heat and then simmer for about 20 minutes, stirring occasionally, until the plums are soft.

Remove the bay leaves, then place the cooked plums in a blender and purée. Return the purée to the pan and add the Madeira, sugar and lemon juice. Bring to the boil, then reduce the heat and simmer for about 30 minutes, stirring frequently.

Spoon the paste into sterilized glass jars, leaving a ¼-inch/5-mm space from the top. Carefully tap them on the counter top to get rid of air pockets. Wipe the jars clean and screw on the lids. Leave to cool. Store in the refrigerator and eat within 1 month.

A Colorful
Palette

A Colorful Palette

Cheeses of many hues

This board is a feast for the eyes as well as the stomach, so choose cheeses that are vibrant and eye-catching. If you want to be the hit of a potluck or bring-a-dish dinner party, then here's your homerun! The goal is to showcase a range of textures and colors so there's plenty of visual diversity. There are countless cheeses out there with exciting, colorful rinds and intriguing shapes—so use this board as a leaping-off point to think about the beauty of cheese. Scour your cheese counter and take advantage of the flamboyant artistry. (But don't forget to take flavors into account, too.)

Cheese Descriptions:

MIMOLETTE (A)
Isigny Sainte-Mère (Normandy, France)
Fondly referred to as the "cantaloupe cheese", this singular cow's milk wheel—with its bright-orange paste and craggy brown rind—is an instant crowd-pleaser. The rind is part of its charm, and the pumpkin-orange interior is boosted by the addition of annatto (a natural dye made from the seed of the achiote tree). Older varieties of mimolette (known as *vieille* or *extra-vieille*) boast a more toothsome texture and a deeper, sharper flavor.
Substitutions: Sparkenhoe Red Leicester (Leicestershire Handmade Cheese; Leicestershire, England), Piacentinu Ennese PDO (multiple producers; Italy), L'Amuse Signature Gouda (IJmuiden & Amsterdam, Holland), Vieux Chimay (Chimay, Hainaut, Belgium).

FLEUR VERTE (B)
La Chèvrefeuille (Perigord, France)
This bright white, soft goat's milk cheese is dusted with vibrant green herbs and pink peppercorns. Fresh, lemony and light, its topping of dried thyme and tarragon adds a delicate, herbaceous backbone. It's easy to spread on everything, from bread to crackers and vegetable crudités.

Substitutions: Tome de Bordeaux (Jean d'Alos; Loire Valley, France), Julianna (Capriole Goat Cheese; Greenville, Indiana, USA), Coeur de la Crème Herbs de Provence (Baetje Farms; Bloomsdale, Missouri, USA), Perroche, herbed (Neal's Yard Creamery; Herefordshire, England), Sussex Slipcote Garlic & Herb (High Weald Dairy; West Sussex, England).

ORIGINAL BLUE (C)
Point Reyes Farmstead Cheese Co. (Tomales Bay, California, USA)
A wedge of this bright white wheel, criss-crossed by lines of azure blue mold, stands out in any setting. A farmstead cheese, it's made from raw cow's milk from a closed herd that grazes the Giacomini family's bucolic pastures. Not only are its colors striking—the flavors command deserved attention, too. Blue lovers will fall for a new crush here. Leftovers? Use them on a steak or burger.
Substitutions: Devon Blue (Ticklemore Cheese; Devon, England), Maytag Blue (Maytag Dairy Farms; Iowa, USA), Yorkshire Blue (Shepherd's Purse; Yorkshire, England), Cashel Blue (JL Grubb; Tipperary, Republic of Ireland), Celtic Blue (Glengarry Fine Cheese; Ontario, Canada).

PIPER'S PYRAMID (D)
Capriole Goat Cheese (Greenville, Indiana, USA)

The lopped pyramid is a traditional shape for certain French goat's milk cheeses—and this take on the classic from Indiana will look unique on your board. A velvety, white rind dusted with smoked paprika protects the bright eye-catching goat's milk paste within. The texture is fudgy, while the flavors are clean yet earthy—and there is a thin line of smoked paprika running through the center, too.

Substitutions: Valençay PDO (multiple producers; Loire Valley, France), Bloomsdale (Baetje Farms; Bloomsdale, Missouri, USA), Cerney Ash (Cerney Cheese; Gloucestershire, England), Tor (White Lake Cheese; Somerset, England).

RED ROCK (E)
Roelli Cheese Haus (Shullsburg, Wisconsin, USA)

The mottled, tan-white natural rind of this rectangular-shaped cheese bears no resemblance to its interior: a vibrant burnt-orange paste jutted with straight lines of blue mold. This twist on a cheddar proves that bright color doesn't equate sharpness; the deep color is thanks to a dose of annatto, and the flavor is mild and creamy. Meanwhile, the blue-green mold *Penicillium roqueforti*—like you'd find in a blue cheese—adds a tinge of piquancy.

Substitutions: Shropshire Blue (multiple producers; Nottinghamshire/Leicestershire, England), Blacksticks Blue (Butler's Farmhouse Cheeses; Lancashire, England).

Suggested Accompaniments

TO BUY IN:

soft fresh bread
plain crackers
mixed olives
small, sweet and mildly hot chilli peppers (such as Peppadew)
caper berries

TO MAKE:

Peppered pan-roasted olives

Jewel-bright and juicy, these bright green Italian Castelvetrano/Nocellara olives will hold their own among the strong colors on your cheese board. Mixed with citrus and salty capers, they counteract the creamy cheeses with bursts of refreshment as you bite into them.

2 tablespoons olive oil
8 oz./225 g unpitted Castelvetrano/Nocellara olives
2 slices of dried tangerine (or orange)
½ teaspoon freshly ground black pepper
2 teaspoons salted capers

SERVES 4–6

Heat the oil in a skillet/frying pan over a medium heat. Add the olives, tangerine (or orange) slices, black pepper and salted capers and fry for 3–4 minutes, stirring occasionally. Tip into a bowl and serve immediately.

CHEESE LIST:

A Mimolette

B Fleur Verte

C Original Blue

D Piper's Pyramid

E Red Rock

They go Together

They go Together

Pairing cheeses and foods

There are no legally binding rules when it comes to pairing, but there is no denying that certain foods marry better than others. To compose a platter of perfect partners, you don't need to come up with something fancy or contrived—simple is very often the way to go. Just let the amalgamation of the cheese and its natural flavor match do the work and keep one basic rule in mind: do not overpower! The cheese and its accompaniment should glide well together, in terms of both flavor and appearance. Quantities can vary—you might serve a few berries alongside one small bite of cheese, for example, but make sure the accompaniment enhances the cheese, and that the cheese raises the accompaniment's merits in turn. Your guests will appreciate the thoughtfulness and diversity as well as the bountiful board.

Cheese Descriptions:

STRACCHINO WITH MORTADELLA (A)
Nonno Nanni (Veneto, Italy)

This soft, gooey and versatile cow's milk cheese is irresistible whether on its own, in a pairing, or as an ingredient in cooking. It is fresh and rindless, so it needs a vehicle to move from board to mouth—and it makes a marvelous addition to a sandwich or pizza, since it spreads and melts beautifully. Mortadella is a thinly sliced meat made from ground, heat-cured pork flavored with spices and dotted with pistachios. Here, the delicate meat and milky cheese match each other in gentleness and texture.
Substitutions: Stracchino (multiple producers; Italy) Crescenza-Stracchino (BelGioioso Cheese; Denmark, Wisconsin, USA), Crescenza (Bellwether Farms; Petaluma, California, USA).

PETITE SUPREME WITH MOSTARDA (B)
Marin French Cheese (Petaluma, California, USA)

This one proves that a diminutive size doesn't diminish flavor. Handmade in the rolling hills of Northern California from local cow's milk, the little white-rinded button is rendered extra-buttery thanks to added cream. Every part of this "triple-cream" is meant to be consumed—including that white "bloomy" rind. And its makers are certified pros: founded in 1865, Marin French Cheese is the longest continuously-operated cheese factory in the US. It pairs well with Mostarda: though it looks like jam, this sweet concoction hides a spicy surprise that hits the palate at the end: hot mustard! Traditionally from northern Italy and made with candied fruits and mustard syrup, this sweet-steamy fruit compote is recreated with mustard powder and adds a glorious kick that balances the richness of the triple-crème cheese and the sweetness of the fruits (fig, quince, pear, etc.).
Substitutions: Eidolon (Grey Barn & Farm; Martha's Vineyard, Massachusetts, USA), Finn (Neal's Yard Creamery; Herefordshire, England), St. Stephen (Four Fat Fowl; Stephentown, New York, USA), Mini Brillat-Savarin (multiple producers; France), Bix (Nettlebed Creamery; Oxfordshire, England).

BUCHETTE WITH FRESH BLUEBERRIES (C)
Laura Chenel's (Sonoma, California, USA)

This little log of goat's milk cheese ripens from the outside-in; the rind becomes wrinkled as it ages while the interior slowly softens. Hand-ladled and delicate, the older the Buchette gets, the stronger its flavors—which are lemony, tangy and perfumed. This version is dusted with vegetable ash; they also offer a non-ashed version. Laura Chenel—who began raising dairy goats in her home state of California in the 1970s and less than a decade later was making cheese for Chez Panisse—is celebrated as the woman who brought commercial goat's cheese production to the US. Simple yet inspired, a blueberry alongside luscious, soft goat's cheese adds a burst of fruit that both cleanses and sweetens the palate. Plus, they are easy to eat and eye-catching.

Substitutions: Sainte-Maure de Touraine PDO (multiple producers; Loire Valley, France), Golden Cross (Golden Cross Cheese; Sussex, England), Driftwood (White Lake Cheese; Somerset, England), Ragstone (Neal's Yard Creamery; Herefordshire, England).

TARENTAISE RESERVE WITH ROASTED NUTS (D)
Spring Brook Farm (Reading, Vermont, USA)

Inspired by Alpine-style cheeses made in France, the original wheels were first produced at Thistle Hill Farm (2002), then neighboring Spring Brook Farm partnered to ramp up production (2008). The cheese is made from the raw milk of the farm's own Jersey cows. The very best wheels—about one in 20—are selected and set aside for longer aging, eventually becoming the "Reserve" version after at least 18 months. The mission-driven oversight of Spring Brook Farm is Farms for City Kids, a non-profit foundation that aligns with inner-city schools to combine first-hand farming experience with classroom studies. The much-lauded cheese tastes of roasted meat and baked bread, and it makes a mouth-watering grilled cheese sandwich. For a classic pairing, the multi-layered flavors in this cheese go perfectly with umami-laden roasted nuts. Always opt for roasted but unsalted nuts when pairing with cheeses—salt is an important ingredient in cheesemaking for controlling moisture, forming the rind and preserving the cheese, so adding more via the accompaniment isn't necessary.

Substitutions: Beaufort PDO (multiple producers; Savoie, France), Gruyère AOP (multiple producers; Switzerland), Pleasant Ridge Reserve (Uplands Cheese; Dodgeville, Wisconsin, USA), Ascutney Mountain (Cobb Hill Cheese; Vermont, USA), Doddington (Doddington Cheese; Northumberland, England), Comté AOP (multiple producers; Jura, France), Louis d'Or (Fromagerie du Presbytère; Centre-du-Quebec, Canada).

STILTON PDO WITH HONEY (E)
Colston-Bassett Dairy (Nottinghamshire, England)

For a cheese to be called "Stilton", it must be made within a strict geographic area in England near a town of the same name. Made from cow's milk, the blue beauty is studded with veining that lends it a marbled look and peppery flavors that marry so well with sweet wines and fruits. This traditional drum-shaped, natural-rinded cheese is undeniably majestic, but it isn't just for holidays: it's classic, and always an excellent choice. There are many different honeys out there, but they all share one thing in common: sweetness. And sweet + cheese = happy. Produced by industrious, single-focused bees, honeys vary depending on the nectar source. For the purposes of pairing with blue cheeses (which are, for the most part, stronger in flavor) go for lighter, floral honeys like wildflower, cherry blossom and clover.

Substitutions: Stichelton (Stichelton Dairy; Mansfield, England), Fourme d'Ambert PDO (multiple producers; France), Bayley Hazen Blue (Jasper Hill Farm; Greensboro, Vermont, USA), Bath Blue (Bath Soft Cheese Co; Somerset, England), Young Buck (Mike's Fancy Cheese; Belfast, Northern Ireland), Bleu d'Elizabeth (Fromagerie du Presbytère; Centre-du-Quebec, Canada).

Suggested Accompaniments

TO BUY IN:

mortadella ham

fresh blueberries

honey or honeycomb

mixed roasted nuts

mostarda or chutney

TO MAKE:

Parmesan pepper shortbreads

These crumbly and peppery shortbreads are great savory little morsels to go with the sweet honey and blueberries on this pairing board.

2 cups/270 g all-purpose/plain flour, plus extra for dusting

1 cup/80 g finely grated Parmesan cheese

2 teaspoons coarsely ground black peppercorns

1 tablespoon fresh thyme leaves

2 sticks/225 g salted butter, chilled and cubed

1 tablespoon coarse sea salt

2 baking sheets, lined with baking parchment

2½-inch/6-cm round cookie cutter

MAKES ABOUT 27

Put the flour, Parmesan, pepper and thyme in a food processor and combine. Add the butter and process until the dough comes together.

Turn the dough out onto a floured work surface and knead for a few minutes, then roll out to a thickness of ¼-inch/5-mm. Cut out rounds using the cookie cutter and place on the prepared baking sheets. Gather up and re-roll the scraps until all the dough has been used. Mark the top of the shortbreads with a fork or leave plain. Place the sheets in the freezer for 15 minutes to chill.

Preheat the oven to 350°F (180°C) Gas 4.

Remove the shortbreads from the freezer. Sprinkle with the salt and bake in the preheated oven for 12–15 minutes until golden brown. Remove from the oven and transfer to a wire rack to cool.

CHEESE LIST:

A Stracchino

B Petite Supreme

C Buchette

D Tarentaise Reserve

E Stilton PDO

Mother Earth

Vegetarian cheese board

Did you know that not all cheeses are suitable for strict vegetarians? Most cheese is coagulated using an ingredient called "rennet." Traditionally, rennet is sourced from the stomach of a young ruminant; it contains an enzyme called chymosin that helps the animal digest its mother's milk by curdling proteins. Just a few drops in a cheese vat quickly does the same, leading to the separation of the curd (solids) from the whey (liquid): a key moment in cheesemaking. Being derived from an animal's stomach, this rennet is not vegetarian—nor is it halal or kosher. But there's some good news for those with dietary restrictions: a similar coagulation can also be achieved from other non-animal based sources. Some traditional cheeses, particularly from Portugal, utilize a rennet derived from thistle flowers. And in the past 20 years, we've seen significant strides in "fermentation-produced chymosin" (FPC), thanks to advances in the ability to isolate chymosin-producing genes from animals and transfer them to fungi, bacteria or yeasts. Today, many cheeses are made using this "microbial" rennet, so strict vegetarians will have little problem satisfying their cravings.

Cheese Descriptions:

TRUFFLE TREMOR (A)
Cypress Grove (Arcata, California, USA)
If you love the mushroomy flavors in cheeses with white, moldy rinds and luscious, earthy pastes, this is going to blow you away. Not only is it dense and creamy, there are flecks of black truffle scattered throughout, which take mushroomy and earthy tastes to another level entirely. This goat's milk cheese is rich and decadent; even those who aren't chèvre lovers will find a reason to like it.
Substitutions: Hudson Valley Truffle (Coach Farm; Pine Plains, New York, USA), Black Truffle Goat Cheese Log (Laura Chenel's; Sonoma, California, USA), Truffle Goat Cheese (Montchevre; Belmont, Wisconsin, USA), Trufflyn (The Cheese Cellar; Worcestershire, England).

RED HAWK (B)
Cowgirl Creamery (Point Reyes Station, California, USA)
The pungent orange-red rind on this small round occurred naturally when the freshly-made wheels were quietly aging on racks in the sea-sprayed air of Tomales Bay, Northern California. Rather than fight nature, Cowgirl Creamery embraced it—and now this meaty, yeasty, beloved cow's milk cheese with a deeply buttery triple-cream interior has an avid following.
Substitutions: Stinking Bishop (Charles Martell & Son; Gloucestershire, England); Golden Cenarth (Caws Cenarth; Pembrokeshire, Wales), Good Thunder (Alemar Cheese; Mankato, Minnesota, USA), Maida Vale (Village Maid Dairy; Berkshire, England).

CABOT CLOTHBOUND (C)
Cabot Creamery & The Cellars at Jasper Hill (Vermont, USA)

For over 15 years, these cellars in Vermont's Northeast Kingdom have received young Cabot Creamery's clothbound cheddars, which are then carefully larded and wrapped with another layer of cheesecloth and aged for 12-plus months. Savory, buttery and with discernible notes of roasted peanuts, this cow's milk cheddar can easily match any beer, cider or larger red wine, but it won't fight with the tannins. The acidic side of the cheese is muted, and a gentle sweetness dominates and lingers.

Substitutions: Clothbound Cheddar (Grafton Village Cheese; Grafton, Vermont, USA), Flagship Reserve (Beecher's Handmade Cheese; Seattle, Washington, USA), Olde Sussex (Traditional Cheese Company; Sussex, England), Cave Matured Cheddar (Cheddar Gorge Cheese Co.; Somerset, England).

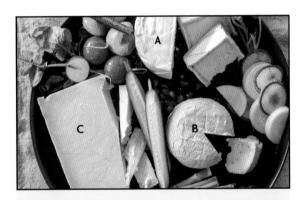

CHEESE LIST:
A Truffle Tremor

B Red Hawk

C Cabot Clothbound

Suggested Accompaniments

TO BUY IN:

fresh vegetable crudités such as asparagus, radishes and mini cucumbers
pomegranate seeds
fresh sage leaves, to garnish

TO MAKE:

Indian spiced apricots

Indian spices give a wonderful balance of tart and sweet with a little heat, which works well with any fruit, especially apricots.

2 cups/400 g superfine/caster sugar
1 tablespoon cardamom pods, bashed
1 teaspoon ground cumin
½ teaspoon chili/chilli powder
¼ teaspoon ground allspice
2 cinnamon sticks
24 fresh apricots
2 large sterilized glass jars with airtight lids

MAKES 4 CUPS (32 FL OZ.)/950 ML

Place the sugar and 4 cups/950 ml of water in a saucepan and bring to the boil over a medium-high heat. Cook for about 8 minutes until the sugar has dissolved. Remove from the heat and stir in the cardamom, cumin, chili/chilli and allspice. Cover and set aside to cool for 15 minutes.

Place a cinnamon stick in each sterilized glass jar. Divide the apricots between the jars, leaving a ¼-inch/5-mm space at the top. Strain the cooled syrup through a fine-mesh strainer/sieve, then pour in over the apricots. Carefully tap the jars on the counter top to get rid of air pockets. Wipe the jars clean and screw on the lids. The apricots will keep for up to 1 month.

With
a Bottle
of Wine

With a Bottle of Wine

Wine-lover's cheese board

When it comes to wine and cheese, palate preferences vary—and this board allows for just that. Rather than focusing on grape variety or location, here, we're pairing according to levels of intensity. You'll still have the progression of lighter to heavier in the cheeses and the wines, but nothing will clash. You might urge your guests to start with the white or rosé, guiding them toward the lighter flavors first. But if they are determined red wine drinkers, that's all good. Enjoying cheese and wine at every level is the point.

Cheese Descriptions:

PASTURES WITH DRY WHITE WINE (A)
Saxon Creamery (Cleveland, Wisconsin, USA)
Made from milk from a single herd of crossed Holstein and high-butterfat Jersey cows, this aged cheddar is bold but buttery, with a creamy sweetness that wraps itself around the wine. It'll make your drink feel appreciated, not overwhelmed. Choose a crisper, less fruit-driven white wine with a touch of minerality; think Muscadet, Vinho Verde, Verdicchio or a lean Sauvignon Blanc.
Substitutions: Raw Cheddar (Organic Pastures; Wisconsin, USA), MontAmoré (Sartori Cheese; Wisconsin, USA), Hafod Welsh Organic Cheddar (Holden Farm Dairy; Ceredigion, Wales).

BURRATA WITH DRY ROSÉ WINE (B)
Di Stefano Cheese (Pomona, California, USA)
This gem contains a hidden treasure: a center filled with shredded pulled curd mixed with cream (also known as *stracciatella*). Well-made burrata begins with fresh, soft cheese curds; it's pulled and formed into a mozzarella-encased pillow of deliciousness by experienced hands. For this pairing, choose a clean, crisp bottle of rosé (rather than a fruit-laden one) and serve it chilled.
Substitutions: Burrata (BelGioioso Cheese; Denmark, Wisconsin, USA), Burrata (Gioia Cheese Co; El Monte, California, USA), Burrata (Maplebrook Farm; North Bennington, Vermont, USA), La Baronia Burrata di Bufala (Caseificio La Baronia; Campana, Italy).

OSSAU IRATY PDO WITH DRY, LIGHT RED WINE (C)
Pyrenees, Hervé Mons (Pays Basque, France)
Aged sheep's milk cheeses from the Pyrenees mountains, home of the culturally-distinct Basque region, are among the best in the world. The dense paste is laden with flavors of grassy pastures, sweet flowers and roasted nuts. The optimum pairing here is a wine that has character and flavor but isn't heavily fruity: a French Pinot Noir or Gamay; an Italian Sangiovese; or something similar.
Substitutions: P'tit Basque (Istara; Pays Basque, France), Esquirrou (Savencia; Pays Basque, France), Berkswell (Berkswell Cheese; West Midlands, England), Spenwood (Village Maid Dairy; Berkshire, England), Corra Linn (Errington Cheese; Lanarkshire, Scotland), Roncal PDO (multiple producers; Navarre, Spain).

PASO VINO WITH HEAVIER RED WINE (D)
Stepladder Ranch & Creamery (Cambria, California, USA)
Since your theme is cheese and wine, why not include

a cheese bathed IN wine? This firm cow's milk wheel has soaked up the grapey flavors of a local Californian Syrah, making it both fruity and sweet. While the Syrah wine is an obvious choice as the drinking partner here, a Cabernet Sauvignon, Merlot, Grenache, Malbec—or a blend— would also pair well with the booze-bathed cheese.

Substitutions: Ubriacco Prosecco (Luigi Guffanti; Arona, Piedmont, Italy), Queso de Murcia al Vino PDO/ Drunken Goat (multiple producers; Murcia, Spain).

ST. AGUR WITH PORT (E)
Savencia Fromage & Dairy (Auvergne, France)

Silky and luscious, this pasteurized cow's milk blue cheese is extremely buttery due to the addition of extra cream. Always a crowd pleaser, St. Agur literally melts in the mouth—and it's easy to spread, too. The blue mold adds a subtle peppery note that doesn't overpower. It's a perfect pairing with sweet port—this rich wine from Portugal is fortified with brandy and comes in several styles, the most popular of which are Ruby (fruit-laden) and Tawny (caramel and roasted nuts). If port isn't available, try

Sauternes, Madeira or Beerenauslese Riesling.

Substitutions: Cambozola Black Label (Käserei Champignon; Bavaria, Germany), Bleubry (Fromagerie Alexis de Portneuf; Quebec, Canada), Kikorangi (Kapiti Cheese; Paraparaumu, New Zealand), Castello Double Crème Blue (Castello Cheese; Midtjylland, Denmark).

Suggested Accompaniments

TO BUY IN:

panforte
chocolate truffles
dry white wine
dry rosé wine
light red wine
heavier red wine
port

TO MAKE:

Candied citrus zest

Store-bought citrus zest has no flavor or aroma in comparison to this delicious homemade version.

zest from 4 oranges, pith removed and cut into matchsticks
3½ cups/700 g superfine/caster sugar
baking sheet, sprinkled with superfine/ caster sugar

MAKES 2 CUPS (16 FL OZ.)/475 ML

Bring a pan of water to the boil and add the orange zest. Cook for 10 minutes, then drain and repeat the process. This will get rid of any bitterness. Set aside.

Bring the sugar and 3 cups/710 ml of water to the boil over a medium-high heat. Reduce the heat and simmer for 5 minutes, stirring occasionally, until the sugar has dissolved. Add the zest and bring to the boil, then reduce the heat to a rapid simmer. Continue to cook for another 20 minutes, brushing down the sides with a pastry brush as necessary. Turn off the heat and allow the citrus zest to cool in the syrup for at least 1 hour.

CHEESE LIST:

A Pastures

B Burrata

C Ossau Iraty

D Paso Vino

E Saint Agur

Preheat the oven to 250°F (120°C) Gas ½.

Remove the zest from the pan with a slotted spoon, shaking any excess syrup back into the pan. Toss the zest in the sugar on the prepared baking sheet and bake in the preheated oven for 45 minutes. Remove from the oven and allow to cool before serving. Store in an airtight container for up to 6 months.

Hops to it

Hops to it

Beer-lover's cheese board

Grain, yeast, water and hops are all relevant when it comes to brewing beer. If any of these ingredients is extra-strident, that will be the key component you'll need to complement with your choice of cheese. Focus on the cheese, and choose the right beer to accommodate its flavors. It's a good idea to arrange your board with the cheeses ranging from lightest to heaviest and have your cheese signs state which beer to pair. Even non-beer drinkers might find a new passion for the brewed beverage with these cheeses.

Cheese Descriptions:

HUMBOLDT FOG WITH WHEAT BEER (A)
Cypress Grove (Arcata, California, USA)

With a velvety mouthfeel and a slightly lemony flavor, this goat's milk cheese is always a hit. It is also beautiful, with a bright white edible rind and a thin, meandering line of vegetable ash running through the paste. Light and refreshing with low hops and hints of clove and tropical fruits, wheat beers are often adorned with a slice of lemon or orange—which mirrors the citrusy tang of this cheese.

Substitutions: Bucheron (multiple producers; Loire, France), Rawstruck (Coach Farms; New York, USA), Selles-Sur-Cher PDO (multiple producers; Loire, France), Ashlynn (The Cheese Cellar; Worcestershire, England).

MATURE CLOTHBOUND CHEDDAR WITH IPA BEER (B)
Quicke's Traditional Cheese Ltd. (Devon, England)

Aged for over 12 months, this is a buttery, intense cow's milk cheddar with undertones of beef broth and hay. Firm and toothsome, it matches a more powerful brew in terms of flavour strength. IPA is known for being a "hoppy" beer, and the hop flower is its bittering agent, which produces aromas ranging from pine to grapefruit, grass and herbs. Paired with robust cheddar, its bitterness steps back, while those secondary aromas leap to the forefront.

Substitutions: Clothbound Cheddar (Shelburne Farms; Vermont, USA), Isle of Mull Cheddar (Sgriob-ruadh Farm; Inner Hebrides, Scotland), Bandaged Cheddar (Bleu Mont Dairy; Wisconsin, USA).

TALEGGIO PDO WITH SAISON BEER (C)
Multiple producers (Lombardy, Italy)

Made into a square shape and washed with a brine to coax out that signature reddish-orange rind, this relatively docile "stinky" cow's milk cheese has been part of Northern Italy's culinary fabric for 1000 years. The edible yeasty rind is crucial to the flavor, especially when paired with beer. Refreshing, spicy, fruity, dry and highly carbonated, saisons are lighter and vary widely. They are a brewers way of showing individual expression.

Substitutions: Livarot PDO (multiple producers; Normandy, France), Aged Brick (Widmer's Cheese Cellars; Theresa, Wisconsin, USA), Chimay Grand Cru (Chimay; Hainaut, Belgium), Ameribella (Jacobs & Brichford Cheese; Connersville, Indiana, USA), Grayson (Meadow Creek Dairy; Galax, Virginia, USA), Durrus (Durrus Cheese; Cork, Republic of Ireland), Merry Wyfe (Bath Soft Cheese Co.; Somerset, England), Oka Classique (Agropur; Quebec, Canada).

CHANDOKA WITH AMBER BEER (D)
LaClare Family Creamery (Malone, Wisconsin, USA)

Made with a blend of cow's and goat's milks, this firm cheese is both sweet and tangy—and slightly addictive. Family-owned, with four of five children employed by the company, LaClare Family Creamery boasts a café, shop and educational tours on cheesemaking. Aptly named because of their copper color, amber beers have a malty, well-balanced sweetness. They gently tame the zing and highlight the milky, creamy flavors in sharper cheeses.
Substitutions: Prairie Breeze (Milton Creamery; Iowa, USA), Cape Meares Cheddar (Tillamook; Oregon, USA), Bandaged Billy (Carr Valley Cheese; Wisconsin, USA).

BARELY BUZZED WITH STOUT (E)
Beehive Cheese (Uintah, Utah, USA)

Made from local cow's milk, this toothsome, full-bodied cheddar is an "American Original". The rind is hand-rubbed with finely ground espresso, lavender and oil, making for a unique and surprisingly good cheese—especially when washed down with the deep, rich flavors

in stout. A dark beer that originally meant "strong" but doesn't necessarily have a high alcohol content. Guinness is one of the most popular stouts, it's lightly sweet with a bitter edge, malty, and smells of roasted coffee beans.
Substitutions: Bellavitano Espresso (Sartori; Monroe, Wisconsin, USA).

Suggested Accompaniments

TO BUY IN:

sourdough bread
wheat beer
IPA beer
Saison beer
amber beer
stout

TO MAKE:

Piccalilli

Served in British pubs alongside a ploughman's lunch, piccalilli goes sublimely with cheese.

1 large cauliflower, chopped into small florets
3 medium zucchini/courgettes, finely diced
2 shallots, thinly sliced
1 medium yellow onion, thinly sliced
3 garlic cloves, finely chopped
⅓ cup/65 g salt
1 tablespoon ground ginger
1 tablespoon ground cumin
1 tablespoon brown mustard seeds
2 tablespoons ground turmeric
2 tablespoons English mustard powder
1 tablespoon chili/chili powder
1 tablespoon curry powder
3 tablespoons cornstarch/cornflour
½ cup/100 g white granulated/caster sugar
2½ cups/600 ml apple cider vinegar
sterilized glass jars with airtight lids

MAKES 8 CUPS (64 FL OZ.)/1.9 L

CHEESE LIST:

A Humboldt Fog

B Quicke's Mature Cheddar

C Taleggio PDO

D Chandoka

E Barely Buzzed

Place the cauliflower, zucchini/courgettes, shallots, onion and garlic in a large bowl. Sprinkle with the salt, cover and set aside for 12–14 hours or overnight.

Rinse the vegetables under cold water and return to the bowl. Place all the rest of the ingredients in a pan and bring to the boil over a medium heat. Turn down the heat and stir the mixture continuously for 3–4 minutes until it thickens. Pour over the vegetables and toss to mix.

Pack the piccalilli into sterilized glass jars, leaving a ¼-inch/5-mm space at the top, and carefully tap the jars on the counter top to get rid of any air pockets. Wipe the jars clean and screw on the lids. Leave to cool. Store in the refrigerator and eat within 1 month.

Apple of my Eye

Cider-lover's cheese board

Fermented apple juice, or "hard" cider, may be the oldest tipple there is—and it's certainly a glorious match with cheese. Taking their well-deserved seats alongside this board of fermented milks are several different ciders in a range of styles. The selections here are meant to express the range of possibilities in this booming category of drink—so it's an excellent opportunity to learn, taste and enjoy. If you love this, think about trying Pommeau or even Calvados sometime. Both are made from apples and are fantastic with cheese, in small doses. A good serving tip is to use different glass types for different ciders, so it's easier to find the suggested pairing.

Cheese Descriptions:

SEASCAPE WITH BRITISH-STYLE CIDER (A)
Central Coast Creamery (Paso Robles, California, USA)
Smooth and toothsome, like perfectly cooked pasta, this cheese is made from a blend of cow's and goat's milks. It has an underlying sweetness that provides a solid foundation, while its light, unobtrusive tanginess keeps you coming back for more. With low carbonation and higher tannins, British-style ciders are made from bittersweet apple varieties rather than those you'll pick up to munch on. The apple flavors are obvious but not cloying with the sweetness of the cheese, and there can be a lemony tartness and a bit of "funk", which is reminiscent of a musty basement (which comes from the yeast).
Substitutions: Mature Plain Gouda (Marieke Gouda; Thorp, Wisconsin, USA), Dutch Girl (Cheeseland; Holland), Lady Prue (Quicke's; Devon, England).

CAMEMBERT WITH FRENCH FARMHOUSE CIDER (B)
Hervé Mons (Normandy, France)
With aromas of sautéed mushroom and shallot and an undertone of earth and orchard, it's easy to understand why this small cow's milk round is made in France's most well-known cider-making region. Close your eyes, savor, and think apple… you might just taste the cider before you even try it. The epicenter of French cider production is Normandy—and this pairing is all about terroir. Redolent with a robust apple flavor yet sparing nothing when it comes to heft, a "cidre de Normandie" stands up to its dairy partner and raises it one, perfectly.
Substitutions: Camembert de Normandie PDO (multiple producers; Normandy, France), Tunworth (Hampshire Cheese; Hampshire, England), Camembert (Le Chatelain; Normandy, France).

FROMAGER D'AFFINOIS WITH MÉTHODE CHAMPENOISE (C)
Fromagerie Guilloteau (Péllusin, Rhône-Alpes, France)
With a butterfat content of at least 60 percent—which makes it a "double cream"—plus a special production technique that creates an extraordinary velvet mouthfeel, this luscious cow's milk cheese is an absolute crowd-pleaser. It is decadent and rich, with floral notes and a creaminess that begs to be cut with a bubbly beverage. There is no reason why bubblies need to be made from

grapes. Exceptional ciders can benefit from secondary bottle fermentation, like that used to make Champagne. The resulting drinks are apple-nuanced and lightly carbonated, perfect partners with cheeses of all kinds—particularly the buttery, creamy beauties like this.

Substitutions: Pavé d'Affinois (Fromagerie Guilloteau; Péllusin, Rhône-Alpes, France), Saint André Fromage (Marquis; Normandy, France), Elmhirst (Sharpham Dairy; Devon, England), Le Riopelle de l'Isle (Fromagerie Ile-Aux-Grues; Quebec, Canada).

CHEESE LIST:

A Seascape

B Camembert

C Fromager d'Affinois

Suggested Accompaniments

TO BUY IN:

pumpernickel bread
raw walnuts
stuffed vine leaves
British-style cider
French farmhouse cider
Méthode Champenoise

TO MAKE:

Provençal olive relish

This is Provence in a jar! The olives are drenched in oil and spiced with capers and salty anchovies. Most ciders marry well with the salt and pungency of this relish.

2 cups/200 g pitted Kalamata olives, drained
12 anchovy fillets
¼ cup/40 g capers, drained
grated zest and freshly squeezed juice of 1 lemon
¼ cup/60 ml extra virgin olive oil, plus extra to cover
cracked black pepper, to taste
sterilized glass jar with airtight lid

MAKES 3 CUPS (24 FL OZ.)/710 ML

Place all the ingredients (except the black pepper) in a food processor and blend until the mixture is almost smooth but still has some texture. Season with black pepper. Pack the tapenade into a sterilized glass jar and drizzle with a little olive oil to cover the surface. Screw on the lid and store in the refrigerator for up to 6 months.

On the Rocks

On the Rocks

Cocktail and cheese pairings

Cheese and cocktails? This concept is considered a novelty—but it works. The anticipation of such a pairing is uplifting and reason enough to throw a party. It's always wise to serve nibbles alongside your drinks, especially with boozy cocktails. Make sure your cocktail recipes are stellar and you've got your best glasses on hand. Also, think ahead: if every guest is having one of each cocktail, you'll need to make sure there are taxis booked or enough beds in the house... because no one will be driving home.

Cheese descriptions:

LA TUR WITH APEROL SPRITZ (A)
Caseificio dell'Alta Langa (Piedmont, Italy)
There are few cheeses with an airy, whipped mousse-esque lightness like this one. A mix of cow's, goat's and sheep's milks, La Tur is a creamy cupcake of lactic heaven. Its wrinkled rind covers a delicate, ivory-colored interior that's soft but not runny. On the palate, it's lightly tangy, like crème fraîche, and slightly floral, like rose petals. The Italian aperitif cocktail, aperol spritz, is made with Prosecco and Aperol (a bitter *aperitivo* liqueur flavored with botanicals and orange). This refreshing drink does not overpower the ultra-creamy cheese and its citrusy backbone pairs well with La Tur's lactic tang.
Substitutions: Robiola di Roccaverano PDO (multiple producers; Piedmont, Italy), Robiola della Rocca (Caseificio dell'Alta Langa; Piedmont, Italy).

PECORINO GINEPRO WITH GIN & TONIC (B)
Salcis (Tuscany, Italy)/Paolo Farabegoli (Emilia-Romagna, Italy)
This cheese hails from the region of Emilia-Romagna, the home of balsamic vinegar in Italy. A firm sheep's milk wheel, it's washed in that local aceto balsamico—along with juniper berries—and aged in oak barrels. The result is a purplish-brown rind tasting of red fruits and pine forest and encasing a bright white, dry and flaky interior, with notes of sour cream. For this pairing, choose a gin with a pronounced juniper flavor; since the cheese itself has been kissed by the plant's berries, it's a logical union.
Substitutions: Balsamic Bellavitano (Sartori Cheese; Plymouth, Wisconsin, USA), Pecorino Ubriaco (La Parrina; Tuscany, Italy).

PLEASANT RIDGE RESERVE WITH A MANHATTAN (C)
Uplands Cheese (Dodgeville, Wisconsin, USA)
Among the most-awarded cheeses in U.S. history, this Alpine-style, raw cow's milk wheel is made only when cows feed on green Wisconsin pastures in summer. Brine-washed and aged on wooden boards for 12 months, it tastes of rich caramel, tropical fruits and beef broth. Comprised of whiskey, sweet vermouth and bitters, the classic Manhattan cocktail is rich and bold, a perfect match for the full-bodied, complex cheese.
Substitutions: Beaufort PDO (multiple producers; Savoie, France), Gruyère AOP (multiple producers; Switzerland), Ascutney Mountain (Cobb Hill Cheese; Vermont, USA), Doddington (Doddington Cheese; Northumberland, England), Comté AOP (multiple producers; Jura, France).

3-YEAR AGED GOUDA WITH A DARK 'N' STORMY (D)
"Vintage Gouda" (Uniekaas, Holland)

Amber-colored and fudgy-textured, studded with crunchy crystals and tasting of butterscotch and browned butter, this is a cheese that keeps on giving. Those sea salt and caramel flavors will linger on your palate and grow, so a little bit goes an extra-long way. Broody yet refreshing, the Dark 'n' Stormy cocktail of ginger beer, rum and a splash of lime is rich, sweet and lingering—just like the gouda.

Substitutions: Noord Hollander (Cheeseland; Holland), Beemster XO (Beemster Cheese; Holland), Berwick Edge (Doddington Dairy; Northumberland, England), Coolea (Coolea Cheese; Cork, Republic of Ireland).

UP IN SMOKE WITH ROSEMARY & GRAPEFRUIT TEQUILA SPRITZ* (E)
Rivers Edge Chèvre (Logsden, Oregon, USA)

Made from farmstead Alpine goat's milk, this soft ball of chèvre is delicious and unique. Maple leaves from the woods adjacent to the Oregon farm are gently smoked over hickory and alder wood chips—as is the cheese

itself—then lightly sprayed with bourbon before being wrapped around the soft goat's milk buttons. There is sweetness from the bourbon, an earthiness from the smoke and a smooth creaminess from the goat's milk. Try it with my recipe for a Rosemary & Grapefruit Tequila Spritz*: soothing aged tequila, zesty grapefruit soda and an extra-herbal kick of fresh rosemary highlight the smoke and cream of the cheese.

Substitutions: This one is an original—but look for fresh cheeses of all milks that have been cold-smoked as a replacement. Alternatively, use a firmer smoked cheese.

Suggested Accompaniments

TO BUY IN:

ingredients for:
Aperol spritz
Gin & tonic
Manhattan
Dark 'n' stormy
Rosemary & Grapefruit Tequila Spritz

TO MAKE:

Spiced & marinated olives

These easy-to-prepare olives are a classic match with any cocktail or cheese.

1 dried red chile/chilli
2/3 cup/90 g Spanish salted Marcona almonds
1 cup/150 g green olives
3 kumquats
1/2 teaspoon cumin seeds
1/4 cup/60 ml Spanish olive oil

MAKES 2 CUPS/300 G

Roughly chop the chile/chilli and the almonds and put them in a bowl with the olives. Thinly slice the kumquats and add to the olive mixture. Sprinkle with cumin seeds, pour over the olive oil, and mix thoroughly. Set aside for at least 1 hour before serving to let the flavors blend.

CHEESE LIST:

A La Tur

B Pecorino Ginepro

C Pleasant Ridge Reserve

D 3-Year Aged Gouda

E Up In Smoke

*Rosemary & Grapefruit Tequila Spritz

4 fl oz./120 ml tequila (I like to use Resposado or Añejo)

1 fl oz./30 ml fresh lime juice

1 sprig of fresh rosemary, plus 2 extra to garnish

6 fl oz./175 ml grapefruit soda

SERVES 2

Add the tequila and lime juice to a cocktail shaker and stir. Pinch off several leaves from the rosemary sprig and muddle into the liquid for several seconds. Add the grapefruit soda, cap and shake. Strain into glasses over ice and garnish each with a rosemary sprig.

TIP: Place a selection of bitters (concentrated botanical flavoring in alcohol) alongside your cheese and cocktail board. Just a few drops of bitters can transform a drink completely. Orange, citrus, basil, rhubarb, smoked chili/chilli, and "aromatic" blends like Peychaud's and Angostura are just a smattering of the many varieties available.

Here Comes the Cake

Cheese wedding "cake"

Make a REAL cheese cake for the big day. Since some prefer cheese over dessert, this growing trend actually makes perfect sense. Use full wheels to build your cake, but make sure that the tiers (at least the top ones) are soft and able to be cut easily—and that the very top tier is small and delicious, and perfect for the bride and groom to set aside for their wedding night. You might want a hands-on cheesemonger with special knives to break down the "cake" for service, or it will get a bit messy. But as long as there is a cake-like look and it can be eaten, that's what matters most. Serve fruit, honey and chocolate alongside and wait for the compliments.

Cheese Descriptions:

COUPOLE (A)
Vermont Creamery (Websterville, Vermont, USA)
This dome-shaped goat's milk cheese with an eye-catching wrinkly rind is a surefire crowd-pleaser. Gently shaped in special forms to capture as much moisture as possible, the texture is delicate and luscious, tasting of buttermilk with a touch of sweet cream. The cheese ages from the outside inward, so the rind will be softer than the center but no less delicious.
Substitutions: Flora (Capriole Goat Cheese; Greenville, Indiana, USA), La Taupinière Charentaise (Fromagerie Jousseaume; Poitou-Charentes, France), Sinodun Hill (Norton & Yarrow; Oxfordshire, England), Damona (Briar Rose Creamery; Dundee, Oregon, USA).

CRÉMEUX DE BOURGOGNE (B)
Fromagerie Delin (Gilly-lès-Cîteaux, Franche-Comté, France)
Produced in the heart of Burgundy by a maker that excels in triple-cream styles, this small, unassuming round is a decadent cow's milk cheese. Made with the addition of extra cream to ensure that it is both luscious and buttery, the Crémeux has a pillowy white rind that's entirely edible. Because this wheel will be supporting weight, ask your cheesemonger to choose one that's not overly ripe (too soft), or else it might turn into a pancake.
Substitutions: Pierre Robert (Fromagerie Rouzaire; Île de France, France), Supreme Brie (Marin French Cheese; Petaluma, California, USA), Brillat-Savarin (multiple producers; Burgundy, France), Triple Rose (Ballylisk; Armagh, Northern Ireland), Vignotte (Fromagerie Raival; Grand Est, France), LaLiberté (Fromagerie du Presbytère; Centre-du-Quebec, Canada).

HUMBOLDT FOG (C)
Cypress Grove (Arcata, California, USA)
Perhaps the most iconic cheese made in the U.S., this goat's milk wheel is also one of the most popular. It comes in two sizes—mini and grande—and both are used here for maximum height and layering. Once it's cut open, a thin line of edible ash running through the cheese is visible, and makes for elegant presentation. Creamy yet slightly crumbly, milky yet slightly tangy, this is a cheese that encourages seconds and thirds.

Substitutions: Délice de Bourgogne, coupe (Fromagerie Lincet; Saligny, France), Cremet (Sharpham; Devon, England), Raven's Oak (Butlers; Lancashire, England).

TIP: If you dare to break further from tradition and want to make sure that the cheese is eaten and truly appreciated, cut the "cake" first to kick off the reception, and use it as the appetizer course. It'll help cut costs as well by serving two purposes.

CHEESE LIST:

A Coupole

B Crémeux de Bourgogne

C Humboldt Fog

Suggested Accompaniments

TO BUY IN:

honey or honeycomb
Turkish delight
fresh fruit such as cherries or wild strawberries
bittersweet/dark chocolate
food-safe roses, to garnish

TO MAKE:

Vine-roasted grapes

These make an elegant, savory-sweet accompaniment for your cheese cake.

1 lb./450 g seedless red grapes on the vine
1 tablespoon extra virgin olive oil
2 teaspoons fennel pollen or ground fennel
1 teaspoon cracked black peppercorns
1 teaspoon coarse sea salt
6 sprigs of fresh thyme

MAKES 1 LB./450 G

Preheat the oven to 375°F (190°C) Gas 5.

Put the grapes in a large, ovenproof dish. Drizzle with the oil, then sprinkle with the fennel, pepper and salt. Gently turn the grapes to coat with the mixture. Place the sprigs of thyme on and around the grapes. Roast in the preheated oven for 45 minutes, turning halfway through. The grapes are best served at room temperature.

Think Local

Cheeses from your own backyard

Because this book was photographed in California, this board's cheeses are all CA-made. The point here is to get to know what is produced locally—the closer, the better. Wherever you are, that's where you need to focus your attention. Diversity on a cheese board is important, so scout out cheeses from different milks and in styles that range in texture and flavor if you can. If not, use what you find and be happy with that. If possible, visit your region's farmers' markets and get to know your local cheesemakers. You'll learn about their products directly, and maybe one day you'll even get to visit the creamery and strike up a friendship over your love of cheese.

Cheese Descriptions:

FIGARO (A)
Andante Dairy (Petaluma, California, USA)
Unwrap the mottled, khaki-to-dark-green-colored fig leaf, and inside you'll find a seasonally-made mixed cow's and goat's milk cheese that's among California's finest. Earthy, fruity and light, the underlying nuttiness in the flavor is reminiscent of coconut milk. Every cheese made by this artisan producer is given a quirky musical name, underscoring the similarities between the art of music and the art of cheesemaking.

RAGGED POINT (B)
Stepladder Creamery (Cambria, California, USA)
This small gem is made from cow's milk, with extra cream added to raise the glorious butterfat to a triple-cream level, producing an extra luscious, buttery cheese. Small, coastal Stepladder Creamery, set halfway between San Francisco and Los Angeles, produces both goat's and cow's milk cheeses, and its three-generation ranch raises heritage pork, Black Angus beef, Haas avocados and fruit.

DREAM WEAVER (C)
Central Point Creamery (Paso Robles, California, USA)
The sticky, orange-tan rind is easy to locate with your eyes closed; just follow your nose. It's yeasty, meaty and funky, which is just what it's supposed to be. Beneath the washed rind, the supple goat's milk cheese is fudgy and dense. This unusual goat's cheese is definitely a hit—just like the '70s song it's named after.

TIP: Some cheese counters have a section devoted to locally-made cheeses and purchase directly from the cheesemakers themselves.

CHEESE LIST:

A Figaro

B Ragged Point

C Dream Weaver

Suggested Accompaniments

TO BUY IN:

fresh local produce of your choice, to go with the local theme

TO MAKE:

Apple, Sage & Calvados paste

Spanish Membrillo paste is famously good with cheese, but quinces can be hard to come by, so this adapted recipe uses apples instead.

6 apples, peeled, cores removed and diced
½ cup/120 ml Calvados or other apple liqueur
2¼ cups/450 g granulated/caster sugar
1 teaspoon dried sage
grated zest and freshly squeezed juice of 1 lemon
sterilized glass jars with airtight lids

MAKES 4 CUPS (32 FL OZ.)/950 ML

Place the apple pieces in a large pan with 3 cups/710 ml of water. Bring to the boil over a medium-high heat. Reduce the heat and simmer for about 45 minutes, stirring occasionally, until the apples are soft.

Place the cooked apples in a blender and purée. Return the purée to the pan and add the Calvados, sugar, sage and lemon zest and juice. Bring to the boil, then reduce the heat and simmer for about 40 minutes, stirring frequently. The paste should be thick and deep in color.

Spoon the paste into sterilized glass jars, leaving a ¼-inch/5-mm space from the top. Carefully tap them on the counter top to get rid of air pockets. Wipe the jars clean and screw on the lids. Keep in the fridge for up to 1 month.

On the Go

Taking cheese on the road

Despite what you might think, cheese is appropriate for a quick meal on the road. It isn't messy, nor is it boring or fussy. In fact, it can be simpler than most meals if you choose the right cheeses. A little refrigerated bag, a plate and a small knife—and you're all set. Don't choose anything overpowering or too potent on the palate or stomach. This board is meant to be simple to assemble and enjoy. Try it on your next work or road trip.

Cheese Descriptions:

ST. ALBANS (A)
Vermont Creamery (Websterville, Vermont, USA)
Everything about this cheese makes it perfect for travel. It comes in its own ceramic crock, and it's easy to scoop out with a small butter knife (it's also a useful size for olive pits after the cheese is gone). Plus, the ethereally light cow's milk cheese pairs well with everything, including fruit and vegetable slices and even chocolate... depending on what your "on the go" snacks of choice look like.
Substitutions: Saint-Marcellin PGI (multiple producers; Rhône-Alpes, France), Saint-Félicien (multiple producers; Rhône-Alpes, France), St. Jude (White Wood Dairy; Suffolk, England).

BRIE (B)
Ferme de la Tremblaye (La Boissière-École, Île de France, France)
Produced on a working farm on the outskirts of Paris, this *fermier* (farmstead) cow's milk cheese is as close to authentic *lait cru* (raw milk) brie as can be found in the U.S. The flavors are earthy and mushroomy with hints of sautéed leeks. There can be flecks of brown or red on the rind, which is natural and should be consumed along with the cheese. You'll just need a cutting surface and a knife.
Substitutions: Brie de Meaux PDO (multiple producers; Île de France, France), Fromage de Meaux (Fromagerie Rouzaire; Île de France, France), Brie de Nangis (Fromagerie Rouzaire; Île de France, France), Baron Bigod (Fen Farm Dairy; Suffolk, England), Sharpham Brie (Sharpham Dairy; Devon, England), Waterloo (Village Maid Dairy; Berkshire, England), Brie (Marin French Cheese; Petaluma, California, USA).

SNOWFIELDS (C)
Saxon Creamery (Cleveland, Wisconsin, USA)
Made with richer late autumn/early winter cow's milk, which is higher in proteins and butterfat, this 6-plus months aged cheese is savory and buttery with lingering flavors of tropical fruits. Its firm-yet-moist paste is studded with small white crystals that develop during the aging process; they provide an addictive crunch.
Substitutions: Butterkäse (multiple producers; Germany and Wisconsin, USA), Toma (Point Reyes Farmstead Cheese; California, USA), Quicke's Buttery Clothbound Cheddar (Quicke's; Devon, England), Cote Hill Yellow (Cote Hill Farm; Lincolnshire, England).

TIP: If your "On the Go" takes you on an airplane, choose a thin-bladed, round-tipped knife that will cut through cheese but isn't dangerous enough to be confiscated.

CHEESE LIST:

A St. Albans

B Brie

C Snowfields

Suggested Accompaniments

TO BUY IN:

red grapes
pita crackers
bittersweet/dark chocolate

TO MAKE:

Garden Patch pickles

I call this "Garden Patch" as these ingredients are very standard vegetables that work well together when pickled. They stand up to strong cheeses and you can easily grab the jar and take them with you "on the go".

a bunch of radishes, halved lengthwise
a bunch of baby carrots
½ cup/50 g pickled cornichons/mini gherkins
1 garlic clove, thinly sliced
3 celery stalks, cut into thirds
1 red onion, sliced
4 Persian cucumbers, quartered
a bunch of pencil-thin asparagus
4 cups/950 ml red wine vinegar
½ cup/100 g brown sugar
1 tablespoon mustard seeds
1 tablespoon fennel seeds
1 tablespoon cumin seeds
1 tablespoon dried rosemary
sterilized glass jars with airtight lids

MAKES 8 CUPS (64 FL OZ.)/1.9 L

Pack all the vegetables into sterilized, size-appropriate glass jars leaving ½-inch/1-cm space at the top.

Put the vinegar, sugar, mustard, fennel and cumin seeds and rosemary in a saucepan and bring to the boil over a medium heat. Turn down the heat and stir for 8–10 minutes until the sugar has dissolved.

Pour the hot vinegar mixture over the vegetables and carefully tap the jars on the counter top to get rid of any air pockets. Wipe the jars clean and tightly screw on the lids. Turn the jars upside down and leave until completely cooled. Store (the right way up) in the refrigerator for at least 24 hours before serving. The pickles can be stored in the refrigerator for up to 2 months.

The Main Course

Cheese for dinner

Do we have to cook to produce dinner? If yes—why? Cheese is a satisfying food and packed with plenty of nutrition. Making a glorious cheese board for dinner is an innovative option, without the fuss. Choose cheeses with staying power that both satiate and leave you wanting more. If you add a hearty pâté such as Pâté de Campagne (a mix of coarsely-ground meat, onions and herbs) and a fresh loaf of bread, even the hungriest eater will be happy. But be careful: this is a board that will fill you up, so be circumspect about how much is consumed. Add a tossed salad with a light dressing for some freshness, and you are good to go.

Cheese Descriptions:

ÉPOISSES DE BOURGOGNE PDO (A)
Hervé Mons Affineur (Burgundy, France)

This "stinky" cheese is blessed with one of the most voluptuous textures of anything out there. Made from cow's milk and washed repeatedly with water and marc (an alcohol distilled from grape pomace), Époisses was first made by monks, who handed the recipe over to local farmers several hundred years ago. The tradition almost died out after WWII, but one maker, Fromagerie Berthaut, kept production going; there are several producers. The yeasts and bacteria that live on the rind make this cheese much-beloved. And the gooey paste beneath, which is silky, rich and spoonable, is almost meat-like in its depth of flavor and umami.

Substitutions: Munster PDO (multiple producers; Alsace/Franche-Comté, France), Rush Creek Reserve (Uplands Cheese; Dodgeville, Wisconsin, USA), Winnemere (Jasper Hills Farm; Greensboro, Vermont, USA), Goddess (Alex James Presents, White Lake Cheese; Somerset, England) Renegade Monk (Feltham's Farm; Somerset England).

GRAND CRU SURCHOIX (B)
Roth Cheese (Monroe, Wisconsin, USA)

There is a reason that Roth makes some of the best Alpine-style cheeses in the U.S.: it is owned by Emmi, an excellent and well-known Swiss cheese producer and affineur. Roth's Grand Cru collection of cheeses—Original, Reserve and Surchoix—are carefully crafted in copper vats and aged on wood boards, as is traditional in Switzerland. The best wheels are chosen for extra-long aging, eventually becoming Surchoix. Complex and savory, with many layers of flavor, you'll discover nuances that keep on surfacing with each bite.

Substitutions: Gruyère AOP (multiple producers; Switzerland), L'Etivaz (multiple producers; Switzerland), Tarentaise (Spring Brook Farm; Reading, Vermont, USA), Little Mountain (Roelli Cheese Haus; Shullsburg, Wisconsin, USA), Le Baluchon (Ste-Anne-de-la-Péracle; Quebec, Canada).

CHEESE LIST:

A Époisses de Bourgogne PDO

B Grand Cru Surchoix

C Evalon

EVALON (C)

LaClare Family Creamery (Malone, Wisconsin, USA)

There is much to love about this firm, raw goat's milk cheese from family-run LaClare Family Creamery. It took a couple of years for the family to nail down the recipe, but its sweet, deeply nutty, earthy flavors come from the quality of the milk and a recipe that fuses an aged gouda style with Parmesan. This is a cheese that lingers on the palate and becomes more complex as it matures.

Substitutions: Black Betty (Fromagerie L'Amuse; IJmuiden and Amsterdam, Holland), Gouda (Marieke; Wisconsin, USA), Killeen Goat Gouda (Killeen Farmhouse Cheese; Galway, Ireland), Payoyo (Queso Payoyo; Andalusia, Spain).

Suggested Accompaniments

TO BUY IN:

pâté de campagne
fresh crusty bread
tossed lightly dressed green salad
heirloom tomato salad
fresh herbs, to garnish

TO MAKE:

Pepper-infused honey

Serve this briny, peppery honey directly drizzled over your cheese or just whisked into the vinaigrette for your accompanying salad.

2 strings of brined green peppercorns (if you can't buy strings of peppercorns, use 2 tablespoons instead)
2 cups/560 g organic wildflower runny honey
sterilized glass jar with an airtight lid

MAKES 2 CUPS/560 G

Place the peppercorns in a sterilized glass jar with a tightly-fitting lid. Pour in the honey and screw on the lid. Leave to infuse for 1 week before using. The longer you leave the honey, the more intense the taste.

Seize the Day

Seize the Day

Cheese for breakfast

If you like toast, butter and jam for breakfast, why not take it one step further and add cheese? With the diversity of styles and milks, you'll find endless options for your breakfast board. Keep in mind that gentler cheeses are a good way to ease into your day, and a touch of savory ham replaces bacon (see page 110, no cooking!). Fresh cheeses, like ricotta, fully embrace fruits, jams and honey, while cultured butter adds depth to an already-beloved ingredient primed for inclusion. Wake up and carpe diem.

Cheese Descriptions:

RICOTTA (A)
Bellwether Farms (Petaluma, California, USA)

Comforting, delicate, seductive, multi-purpose: these are the words that encapsulate sweet, cream-laden ricotta. Meaning "recooked" in Italian because it is made from reheating the whey left over after cheesemaking, ricotta is normally produced using whole cow's or sheep's milk. At any time, it is a soothing snack, but for breakfast, it gets the belly and body ready for the day ahead—especially when topped with a light drizzle of honey.

Substitutions: Requesón (multiple producers; Spain), Crowdie (multiple producers; Scotland), Quark (multiple producers; Germany).

CASATICA DI BUFALA (B)
Caseificio Quattro Portoni (Lombardy, Italy)

Rich, extra-creamy water buffalo's milk is transformed into this pillow of bone-white cheese, with a custard-like inside texture and a barely discernable rind. The flavors are delicate and milky, with a long-lasting, sweet, buttery finish. This Italian creamery has its own herd of buffalo, whose high-butterfat milk produces very creamy, decadent cheeses.

Substitutions: Stracchino (multiple producers; Italy), Franklin's Teleme Cheese (Los Banos, California, USA), Inglewhite Buffalo Cheese (Carron Lodge; Lancashire, England), The Figaro (Glengarry Fine Cheese; Canada).

COMTÉ AOP (C)
Essex St. Cheese (Jura, France)

Although every wheel of Comté AOP has its own unique flavor spectrum, each producer making it must adhere to the same set of strict rules, which govern everything from permitted cow breeds and amount of fresh forage to the distance between the farmer and cheesemaker. Ranging in taste from cut grass to browned butter, roasted peanuts, raw cashews and even sautéed cauliflower, this raw cow's milk cheese is unceasingly multi-dimensional.

Substitutions: Alpha Tolman (Jasper Hill Farm; Greensboro, Vermont, USA), Beaufort PDO (multiple producers; Savoie, France), Cornish Kern (Lynher Dairies; Cornwall, England).

BEURRE DE BARATTE (CULTURED BUTTER) (D)
Rodolphe Le Meunier (Tours, France)

Not a cheese exactly, but in the dairy family and so perfect for a breakfast board. Historically, the cultures were live bacteria that would proliferate in fresh milk if it were left to ferment, causing cream to float to the top that could be churned into butter. In most of today's cultured butter production, a similar fermentation occurs thanks to a starter culture added directly to cream. This results in a very rich butter, with a light tang that's akin to buttermilk. It is usually available both salted or unsalted.

Substitutions: Isigny Ste. Mère (France), Vermont Creamery (Vermont, USA), Organic Valley (Wisconsin, USA), Bungay Butter (Fen Farm Dairy; Suffolk, England).

COUNTRY HAM
Lady Edison Pork (Chapel Hill, North Carolina)
Highly marbled and with a deep umami flavor that comes from heritage pig breeding and an 18-month aging period, this is a ham that declares its place on your breakfast table.

Substitutions: Jambon de Bayonne PGI (France), Prosciutto di Parma PDO (Italy), Jamón Ibérico PDO (Spain).

CHEESE LIST:

A Ricotta

B Casatica di Bufala

C Comté PDO

D Beurre de Baratte (cultured butter)

Suggested Accompaniments

TO BUY IN:

country ham (see left)
fresh baguettes
fresh fruit, such as blackberries and apricots
honey and/or jam

TO MAKE:

Italian flatbread with tomatoes

This Italian-style flatbread has a simple topping of roasted cherry tomatoes, perfect for breakfast.

1¾ cups/225 g all-purpose/plain flour
1 teaspoon dried hot pepper/chilli flakes
1 teaspoon sel gris
⅔ cup/150 ml of warm water
2 tablespoons olive oil, plus extra to brush and drizzle
1½ teaspoons fast-action dried yeast
¼ teaspoon brown sugar
1 cup/150 g cherry tomatoes
3–4 fresh rosemary sprigs
3 tablespoons olive oil
2 tablespoons each dried basil and dried parsley
cracked black pepper and fleur de sel, to season

SERVES 4

Mix the flour, hot pepper/chilli flakes and salt in a food processor. Put the warm water, oil, yeast and brown sugar in a pitcher/jug and add the liquid to the flour in a steady stream. Process for about 3 minutes until the dough forms a ball. Transfer to a floured surface and knead for about 3 minutes. Transfer to an oiled bowl, cover and leave in a warm place until doubled in size.

Preheat the oven to 475°F (240°C) Gas 9.

Roll the dough into a long oval and prick all over with a fork. Mix together the tomatoes, rosemary and 3 tablespoons oil. Brush the dough with oil and top with the tomato mixture and season. Transfer to a baking sheet and bake in the preheated oven for 15 minutes or until the dough is crisp. Sprinkle with the herbs, pepper and salt and drizzle with olive oil to serve.

Go Fly a Kite

A cheese picnic

Spread the blanket and place down the board—cheese somehow tastes better at a picnic. Consider, though, where you will be and what the weather will be like. If it's sunny and warm (two things that cheeses aren't keen on), avoid wedges that will "sweat" profusely and cheeses with a high butterfat content. Also steer clear of "stinky" cheeses; they are prone to attract insects. Otherwise, all is fair for picnic fare. For ease of serving and eating, pre-cut each wedge into bite-size pieces, leaving the rind on.

Cheese Descriptions:

APPLE WALNUT SMOKED (A)
Beehive Cheese (Uintah, Utah, USA)
Walnut shells and apple slices are the base of a cold smoke that permeates this firm cow's milk cheddar-style cheese. Smooth-textured and sweet, yet savory with a light tang, the cheese's soft smokiness lends itself to a picnic in the great outdoors—with or without a campfire.
Substitutions: Apple Smoked Cheddar (Carr Valley Cheese; Wisconsin, USA), Smoked Cheshire (Appleby's; Shropshire, England), Oak-Smoked (Northumberland Cheese Co.; Newcastle upon Tyne, England), Smoked Lincolnshire Poacher (Lincolnshire Poacher Cheese; Lincolnshire, England), Smoked Westcombe Cheddar (Westcombe Dairy; Somerset, England), Idiazabal (multiple producers; Basque Country, Spain), (COWS Creamery; Charlottetown, Prince Edward Island, Canada).

GRANQUESO (B)
Roth Cheese (Monroe, Wisconsin, USA)
Inspired by Spanish cheeses made traditionally in a woven basket, this firm cow's milk wheel has a sunset-orange, herringbone rind rubbed with cinnamon and paprika that permeates the paste. Savory yet buttery with a hint of sweetness, it's easy to keep nibbling on.

Substitutions: Manchego PDO, semi-curado (multiple producers; Castilla-Leon, Spain), Mahón PDO (multiple producers; Menorca, Spain), Ibérico (multiple producers; Castilla-Leon, Spain).

MIDNIGHT MOON (C)
Cypress Grove (Arcata, California, USA)
Sweet, toothsome and satisfying, this goat's milk gouda (made in Holland from a recipe perfected by California's Cypress Grove) is both approachable and crowd-pleasing. Its dense, fudgy texture is easy to cut and savor, with flavors of white chocolate, warmed milk and a rich, lingering sweetness that melts on the palate.
Substitutions: Dutch Girl (Cheeseland; Holland), Goat Gouda (Central Coast Creamery; California, USA), Brabander (Fromagerie l'Amuse; IJmuiden and Amsterdam, Holland).

CHEESE LIST:

A Apple Walnut Smoked

B GranQueso

C Midnight Moon

Suggested Accompaniments

TO BUY IN:

whole-wheat crackers
blood oranges and/or tangerines
nuts and fruits in honey
dried figs

TO MAKE:

Pickled strawberries & grapes

It's easy to over-buy at the farmers' market, especially in summer when the stalls are weighed down with plump, juicy fruits and berries. These sweet and sharp pickled strawberries and grapes are a good way to make use of excess produce, and they add a nice touch to your summery cheese picnic.

For the Pickled Strawberries

24 strawberries, plus some leaves (optional)
1 cup/235 ml white balsamic vinegar
2 tablespoons kosher salt
2 tablespoons white sugar
1 tablespoon pink peppercorns

For the Pickled Grapes

2 cups/5½ oz red seedless grapes
1 cup/235 ml apple cider vinegar
1 tablespoon turbinado/demerara (or light brown) sugar
1 teaspoon kosher salt
1 fresh red chile/chilli
sterilized glass jars with airtight lids

SERVES 6–8

To make the pickled strawberries, pack them, and the leaves if using, into a sterilized jar with a tight-fitting lid. Place the vinegar, salt, sugar and peppercorns in a pan with ¼ cup/60 ml of water and bring to the boil over a medium-high heat. Cook for 3 minutes, then pour over the strawberries. Set aside to cool, then screw the lid on tightly and refrigerate overnight before serving.

To make the pickled grapes, pack the grapes into a sterilized jar with a tight-fitting lid. Place the vinegar, sugar and salt in a pan with ¼ cup/60 ml of water and bring to the boil over a medium-high heat. Cook for 3 minutes, then pour over the grapes and add the red chile/chilli to the jar. Set aside to cool, then screw the lid on tightly and refrigerate overnight before serving.

Cheese Plus Meat

Cheese Plus Meat

Charcuterie meets its soulmate

There's a reason most cheese shops sell cured meats and pâtés, and many restaurants include them on their cheese boards: they not only complement each other in taste (especially umami), they also provide a depth of varying textures and colors. So, don't forget about the meat! In fact, highlight both of these fantastic food groups by placing them together and letting your board's flavors tell their stories. When pairing, there are few missteps—except for when there are flavorings in the meats or cheeses that might conflict or overpower. When in doubt, go neutral.

Cheese Descriptions:

ASIAGO PDO MEZZANO (A) WITH SPECK ALTO ADIGE PGI, Agriform (Trentino/Veneto, Italy)

This semi-firm cow's milk cheese comes from the alpine Asiago Plateau, that spans four provinces in northeast Italy. The Po river irrigates the wide, fertile valley that abuts the mountainous region to the northeast where the Adige river flows. *Mezzano* ("middle") versions are aged for around four months, resulting in a cheese that is pliable and light yellow, with subtle milky flavors. Produced in the same general vicinity, Speck Alto Adige PGI is a terroir-based match. This dry-cured, lightly smoked ham from South Tyrol in Italy is produced using salted pork thighs seasoned with a mix of spices (pepper, rosemary, juniper, bay) and then smoked. Producers adhere to the "a little salt, a little smoke and a lot of fresh air" method, with air being as much a factor as the other ingredients.
Substitutions: Havarti (multiple producers; Denmark, Wisconsin, USA), São Jorge PDO, 3-month (multiple producers; Azores, Portugal), Mayfield (Alsop & Walker; East Sussex, England), Vacherin Fribourgeois (multiple producers; Switzerland), Ogleshield (Montgomery's; Somerset, England), Fontina PDO (multiple producers; Aosta Valley, Italy).

PIAVE PDO VECCHIO (B) WITH PROSCIUTTO DI PARMA PDO, Lattebusche (Veneto, Italy)

Named after the Piave river, which flows through the stunning Dolomites region of Italy it calls home, this hard cow's milk cheese is made with milk sourced solely from the province of Belluno. The wheel is aged for over 12 months (*vecchio* is the term used for aged versions; there are younger versions with different texture and flavor profiles) and it is both bright and lightly sweet, with intense pineapple and tropical fruit flavors. To go with this: soft ribbons of sliced Prosciutto di Parma. A pork leg from a well-cared-for pig, sea salt and aging in a quiet, dark, humidity-controlled environment for at least 18 months, leads to the sweet, perfumed flavors in this meat.
Substitutions: Bra Duro PDO Vecchio (multiple producers; Italy), Lincolnshire Poacher (Lincolnshire Poacher Cheese; Lincolnshire, England), SarVecchio Parmesan (Sartori; Wisconsin, USA), American Grana (Belgioioso; Wisconsin, USA), Cornish Kern (Lynher Dairies; Cornwall, England), Parmigiano Reggiano PDO (multiple producers; Emilia-Romagna, Lombardy, Italy).

CACIO DE ROMA FRESCO (C) WITH FINOCCHIO SALAMI, Caseificio Santa Maria (Rome, Italy)

There is little more comforting than a semi-soft, silky sheep's milk cheese, and this is one not to miss. Made in the outskirts of Rome, this small round boasts extra-milky, lusciously creamy flavors that keep you coming back for more. And if there are leftovers, try thin slices atop pizza or grate some over hot pasta. Wild fennel grows all over the Mediterranean, and this uncured, Tuscan-style pork salami (from Salumeria Beillese in New York) transports you there. Although subtle, the deeply herbal, anise notes that come from the fennel seed and fennel pollen incorporated into the salami are decisive, yet they cozy up well to the mellow cheese.

Substitutions: Pecorino Fresco (multiple producers; Italy), Manchego Fresco PDO (multiple producers; La Mancha, Spain), Duddleswell (High Weald Dairy; West Sussex, England).

LEONORA (D) WITH BRESAOLA
Facendera (León, Spain)

With its undeniably lemony tang and fudgy texture, this goat's milk cheese is bright white, cakey and dense. It is made into an unusual rectangular loaf shape and cut into vertical pieces so it's easy to see the cream line underlying the white-molded rind. Delicious at all levels of ripeness, Leonora's flavors grow stronger as it ages—with the rind becoming the most intense. Bresaola is a very lean meat that complements the goat's milk cheese beautifully. It is made with a carefully trimmed leg of beef, dry-rubbed with salt and spices (ranging from nutmeg to black pepper and juniper berries) and then given a prolonged drying period. Serve it thinly sliced and don't leave it out long before serving.

Substitutions: Bûcheron (multiple producers; Loire, France), Sofia (Capriole Goat Cheese; Greenville, Indiana, USA), Monte Enebro (Queserías Tietar; Castilla-Leon, Spain), White Nancy (White Lake Cheese; Somerset, England).

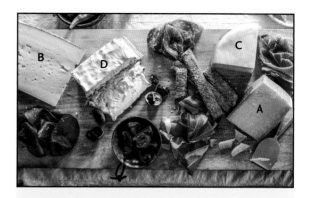

CHEESE LIST:

A Asiago Mezzano PDO

B Piave Vecchio PDO

C Cacio de Roma, fresco

D Leonora

Suggested Accompaniments

TO BUY IN:

speck Alto Adige PGI

prosciutto di Parma PDO

finocchio Salami

bresaola

sundried tomatoes

pickled okra

red walnuts

TO MAKE:

Rainbow pepper oatcakes

A wonderful Scottish classic, oatcakes are lovely to serve with cheese and cured meats. You can cut the dough into strips, triangles or squares, or use cookie cutters.

2½ cups/235 g old fashioned/rolled oats

2 teaspoons cracked rainbow peppercorns

2 teaspoons coarse sea salt

½ teaspoon baking soda/bicarbonate of soda

2 tablespoons melted butter

1 cup/235 ml boiling water

2 baking sheets, lined with baking parchment

MAKES ABOUT 15

Preheat the oven to 350°F (180°C) Gas 4.

Put the oats, peppercorns, salt and baking soda/ bicarbonate of soda in a food processor and pulse to mix. Pour in the melted butter and boiling water and process until a dough begins to form.

Turn the dough onto a floured work surface. Roll out to a long rectangle 6 inches/15 cm wide, then cut into strips 1 inch/2.5 cm wide and lay on the prepared baking sheets. Bake in the preheated oven for 15–18 minutes until golden brown, then cool on wire racks before serving.

Showstopper

Showstopper

Get your camera ready!

Sometimes you need to make a statement. This is that moment! Scour your cupboards and pull out those jars you've been keeping in the back of the fridge. Creativity craves innovation—and abundance, color, contrasting textures and thoughtful pairings lead to a board that will elicit gasps and "aahs". Have everything you want on the board open and ready before you start, and generally map out where each cheese will go and how much space it will need. Then dive in, working from the center outward, using the accompaniments as frames highlighting the cheeses. Keep in mind that this is not simply about design but also practicality; this board will be devoured. Make every beautiful inch accessible to the hungry cheese lovers. But at the same time don't let pragmatism dampen your creativity.

Cheese Descriptions:

ALP BLOSSOM (A)
Sennerei Huban (Vorarlberg, Austria)
This cow's milk cheese is dense and firm, with long-lasting flavors of roasted nuts, boiled milk and beef. And then there is that glorious rind, coated with Alpine flowers and herbs, which are not only edible but add subtle, delicate flavors. This is a showstopper in itself.
Substitutions: Hudson Flower (Old Chatham Sheepherding/Murray's Cheese; New York, USA), Buchette aux Fleurs (Fromagerie Jacquin; La Vernelle, France).

10-YEAR CHEDDAR (B)
Hook's Cheese Company (Mineral Point, Wisconsin, USA)
Moist and slightly crumbly, with pockets of crunchy crystals, the flavors of this decade-long-aged cow's milk cheddar are complex but stay true to its style. It is savory and lemony in taste, begging you to take another mouthful. The vibrant orange color comes from the addition of annatto (a natural food coloring) and brightens up any cheese board.

Substitutions: Extra Sharp Cheddar, Yellow (Cabot Creamery; Cabot, Vermont, USA), 10-Year Extra Sharp Cheddar (Henning's Cheese; Kiel, Wisconsin, USA).

BIJOU (C)
Vermont Creamery (Websterville, Vermont, USA)
Meaning "jewel" in French, this tiny button of hand-shaped goat's milk cheese with its wrinkled, soft rind and dense center, can be tucked into creative spaces on the board. It is delicate and mild, with flavors of yeast, sweet flowers and freshly cut hay.
Substitutions: Crottin de Chavignol PDO (multiple producers; Loire, France), Kunik 'mini' (Nettle Meadow Farm; Warrensburg, New York, USA), Chabichou de Poitou PDO (multiple producers; Loire, France).

OVELHA AMANTEIGADO (D)
Queijos Tavares (Beira Alta, Portugal)
Circled with a white cotton strip for support, this raw sheep's milk wheel is unique both in look and taste and is

soft enough to be spooned out of its rind like "soft butter" (amanteigado). Made using plant-based traditional thistle rennet to coagulate the milk, the wheel boasts grassy, tangy flavors and an irresistible creaminess.

Substitutions: Queijo Serra da Estrela PDO (multiple producers; Portugal), Zimbro (Casa Lusa; Portugal), Quiejo de Azeitão PDO (multiple producers; Portugal), Torta del Casar PDO (multiple producers; Extremadura, Spain),Torta de Finca Pascualete (Finca Pascualete; Extremadura, Spain).

GARROTXA (E)
Sant Gil d'Albió (Catalonia, Spain)

A thin, dark gray rind protects a chalk-white paste, which is tender, toothsome and velvety. This firm goat's milk cheese is versatile and imminently likeable, with herbal notes and a sweet, milky finish. Its traditional recipe had almost disappeared by the 1980s, when a young cheesemaker and goat cooperative brought it back.

CHEESE LIST:

A Alp Blossom

B 10-year Cheddar

C Bijou

D Ovelha Amanteigado

E Garrotxa

Now, beautiful versions are made throughout the region. **Substitutions:** Tomme de Chèvre (multiple producers; Savoie, France), Queso de Mano (Haystack Mountain Cheese; Longmont, Colorado, USA), Caprino Stagionato (Marcelli Formaggi; Italy), Innes Burr (Innes Cheese; Staffordshire, England), Brinkburn (Northumberland Cheese Company; Northumberland, England).

Suggested Accompaniments

TO BUY IN:

Parmesan wafers

bread twists

wafer crackers

Corsican olives

fresh fruit such as baby apples, apricots, blackberries and pomegranates

dried lemons

dates

candied orange zest

roasted grapes

tomato jam

TO MAKE:

Rioja & allspice pears

The Rioja wine gives a dark, intense color to these pears as well as a robust and pleasing taste. Allspice brings all of the flavors together, making them a spectacular addition to any cheese board.

3 cups/710 ml Rioja
1 cup/200 g brown sugar
1 tablespoon allspice
grated zest of 1 orange
8 firm pears, cut into quarters and cored
sterilized glass jars with airtight lids

MAKES 8 CUPS (64 FL OZ.)/1.9 L

Pour the Rioja into a saucepan and add the sugar, allspice, and orange zest. Bring to the boil over a medium-high heat. Reduce the heat and simmer for 10 minutes, stirring occasionally until the sugar is completely dissolved. Add the pears to the pan and cook gently for 5 minutes. Remove the pears with a slotted spoon and pack into glass jars, leaving a ¼-inch/5-mm space at the top.

Pour the hot Rioja syrup over the fruit and carefully tap the jars on the counter top to get rid of air pockets. Wipe the jars clean and screw on the lids. Seal the jars. The pears will keep for up to 1 month.

Just the Two of Us

Just the Two of Us

Romance with cheese

Sharing cheese is romantic, especially when paired with a beverage that hugs it. For the perfect romance, choose something that isn't too strong (on the palate or the nose), is easily shareable (less is more), has a luscious texture (gooey and delicious) and can sit out for hours without mishap. Few accompaniments are needed if the cheese is perfectly ripe. Make sure to serve it at room temperature and peel off the top rind so it's both accessible and inviting. True love should never be standoffish.

Cheese Descriptions:

RUSH CREEK RESERVE
Uplands Cheese (Dodgeville, Wisconsin, USA)

When cows are moved indoors in the autumn and start eating dry hay instead of green pasture, their milk becomes richer. That's why Uplands Cheese—makers of Pleasant Ridge Reserve, a firm, raw cow's milk, Alpine-style cheese produced from May to October—switches to this soft, washed rind, raw cow's milk wheel in the autumn and early winter. The cheese is surrounded by a belt of spruce bark and is gently brine-washed, flipped and aged for two months before leaving the creamery.

Substitutions: Vacherin du Haut-Doubs/Mont d'Or PDO (France/Switzerland), Winnemere or Harbison (Jasper Hill Farm; Vermont, USA), Chuefladae (Sepp Barmettler; Nidwalden, Switzerland), Winslade (Hampshire Cheeses; Hampshire, England), Humming Bark (Carrigbyrne Farmhouse Cheese; Wexford, Ireland), Louis d'Or (Fromagerie du Presbytère; Centre-du-Quebec, Canada).

Suggested Accompaniments

TO BUY IN:

red wine

pistachio nougat

candied figs

TO MAKE:

Mexican chili chocolate truffles

A spicy taste from south of the border, these salty chile/chilli chocolate truffles, rolled in Mexican Ibarra chocolate and Himalayan pink rock salt, are divine! You won't be able to stop eating them. Mexican Ibarra chocolate discs are made with chocolate mixed with cocoa beans and cinnamon. Buy them at Latin food markets.

8 oz./225 g bittersweet/dark chocolate (70% cocoa solids), roughly chopped

¼ cup/60 ml pouring cream

1 tablespoon/15 g unsalted butter

½ teaspoon confectioners' chili/chilli oil

3 oz./85 g Ibarra chocolate discs, roughly chopped

1 tablespoon Himalayan pink rock salt

melon baller

MAKES ABOUT 40

Put the chopped chocolate, cream and butter in a heatproof bowl. Place over a pan of simmering water, making sure the water does not touch the bottom of the bowl. Once the chocolate has started to melt, stir gently until the mixture is smooth and creamy.

Stir in the chili/chilli oil and pour the mixture into a shallow bowl. Refrigerate until firm.

Rush Creek Reserve

To make the dusting powder, process the Ibarra chocolate to a powder in a food processor. Pour it into a bowl and mix in the Himalayan salt.

When the chocolate mixture has set, scoop out the truffles with the melon baller and roll into balls. Toss in the dusting powder to coat and serve.

TIP: If you can't find Ibarra chocolate, you can make a similar dusting powder by mixing the following ingredients together: $\frac{1}{3}$ cup/55 g white sugar, $\frac{1}{3}$ cup/30 cocoa powder, 1 teaspoon ground cinnamon and 1 tablespoon Himalayan pink rock salt.

Under the Stars

Camping with cheese

Tucking into a great cheese board surrounded by nature places you in that most enviable position of living in the moment and doing it in style. Every camping trip is different but, in general, you'll want to choose cheeses that travel well (more aged) and that you can savor (long flavors), so you can have them for several days. Store them in airtight plastic bags to keep the scents contained. And if there is a stream nearby, immerse the sealed bags underwater, gently weighted by stones, to keep the cheeses "refrigerated".

Cheese Descriptions:

JEFFS' SELECT GOUDA (A)
Caves of Faribault (Faribault, Minnesota, USA)
A collaboration between two Jeffs—the cheesemaker in Wisconsin and the affineur (ager) in Minnesota—resulted in this cow's milk gouda tasting of butterscotch and roasted nuts. Aged for 12 months in humid sandstone caves that span roughly an acre of land, the wheels are then rubbed with annatto, producing an enticing burnt orange-colored rind. This is a cheese that's easy to enjoy anywhere—especially under the stars.
Substitutions: Gouda Overjarige (Marieke Gouda; Thorp, Wisconsin, USA), Wilde Weide (Fromagerie L'Amuse; IJmuiden and Amsterdam, Holland), Roomano Pradera (Cheeseland; Holland), Mature Cornish Gouda (Cornish Gouda Company; Cornwall, England), Remeker (De Groote Voort; Lunteren, Netherlands), Beemster Classic (Beemster Cheese; Holland), The Lankaaster (Glengarry Fine Cheese; Lancaster, Ontario, Canada).

DRY JACK (B)
Vella Cheese Company (Sonoma, California, USA)
This version of Monterey Jack, a cow's milk cheese originally developed in Monterey, California, is extra-aged (24 months), resulting in a hard, dense wheel that's perfect for snacking, grating, shaving and nibbling. The edible rind is coated with a mixture of cocoa and oil, and the cheese itself is nutty yet not overly rich.
Substitutions: Dry Jack (Rumiano Cheese; Crescent City, California, USA), Piave Vecchio PDO (multiple producers; Veneto, Italy), SarVecchio Parmesan (Sartori; Plymouth, Wisconsin, USA), Mahon PDO, aged (multiple producers; Menorca, Spain), Sao Jorge PDO (multiple producers; Portugal & Azores).

ESTERO GOLD RESERVE (C)
Valley Ford Cheese (Valley Ford, California, USA)
Made from unpasteurized Jersey cow's milk from the farm's own herd (most of which is sold as fluid milk), this firm, crystalline cheese pays homage to the Swiss-Italian roots of the maker's family, who moved to Northern California at the turn of the century. Intense and lingering from its 18 months of aging, the flavors range from stone fruit to brown butter.
Substitutions: Montasio PDO (multiple producers; Friuli, Italy), Asiago Stagionato PDO (multiple producers; Trentino/Veneto, Italy), Cornish Kern (Lynher Dairies; Cornwall, England), Knuckle Duster (Lincolnshire Poacher Cheese; Lincolnshire, England).

CHEESE LIST:

A Jeffs' Select Gouda

B Dry Jack

C Estero Gold Reserve

Suggested Accompaniments

TO BUY IN:

fig & walnut cake
cheese straws
raisin crackers
olives

TO MAKE:

Cherry & rose geranium spoon fruit

Rose geranium leaves lightly perfume this delicious cheese condiment, but you can leave them out if you prefer. Small jars of this are perfect for taking on your next camping trip.

1 cup/200 g granulated/caster sugar
3⅓ cups/450 g firm cherries, rinsed and pits/stones removed
the sprigs and flowers of 1 rose geranium
1 tablespoon freshly squeezed lemon juice
sterilized glass jars with airtight lids

MAKES 2 CUPS (16 FL OZ.)/475 ML

In a pan, bring the sugar and ½ cup/120 ml of water to the boil over a medium-high heat. Reduce the heat and simmer for 8 minutes, stirring occasionally until the sugar is completely dissolved. Add the cherries, gently stir, and simmer for 2 minutes. Remove the cherries with a slotted spoon, shaking any excess syrup back into the pan.

Spoon the cherries into sterilized glass jars, leaving 1/4-inch/5-mm space at the top. Rub the geranium leaves between your fingers to release the oils, then add them to the pan with the syrup. Add the lemon juice and bring to the boil. Continue to cook for about 10 minutes until the syrup becomes thick and reduces slightly. Remove from the heat and discard the geranium leaves.

Pour the hot syrup over the cherries and carefully tap the jars on the counter top to get rid of air pockets. Wipe the jars clean and screw on the lids. The spoon fruit will keep for up to 1 month.

Got Your Goat

All-goat's milk cheese board

This all-goat board is an eye-opener for those who only know spreadable, fresh chèvre as goat's cheese. Chèvre is, of course, goat's milk cheese in its simplest form, but there are so many more styles of goat's cheese out there, it would be a shame to miss out on them. Throughout this book there are plenty of additional examples of goat's cheeses that you can add to diversify your board, so use this spread as an excuse for a delicious adventure. Goat's milk tastes as clean and fresh as cow's milk; it does not have musty or soapy flavors. If it does, it normally means that the milk has been overly agitated during the cheesemaking, damaging delicate fat globules to release potent fatty acids. Generally, cow's and goat's milks are fairly similar in terms of butterfat and lactose contents, but the proteins in goat's milk are different. Finally, the milk itself is chalk-white—without beta-carotene—a good tip for the "guess what cheese this is?" game.

Cheese Descriptions:

WABASH CANNONBALL (A)
Capriole Goat Cheeses (Greenville, Indiana, USA)
On a derelict farm in Indiana, Judy and Larry Schad set up home and began accumulating dairy goats. About a decade later, in 1988, they started making commercial cheese in a neighbor's facility and in a few years had built their own small creamery. Now, 30 years later, they are still producing fine goat cheeses on the farm, including this "American Original". It's hand-shaped into a ball, left to dry for a day, coated with vegetable ash, then aged for about a week. A welcomed white mold grows on the rind before it is shipped for sale. As it ages, its wrinkled exterior becomes more pronounced and its flavors throughout grow more complex.
Substitutions: Chabichou de Poitou PDO (multiple producers; Loire, France), Coupole (Vermont Creamery; Websterville, Vermont, USA), Dorstone (Neal's Yard Creamery; Herefordshire, England).

CABRICHARME (B)
La Fermière de Méan (Ardennes, Belgium)
This semi-soft, raw goat's milk round is made at a dairy cooperative that works exclusively with organic milk. The combo of goat's milk and a washed rind is unusual; as Cabricharme ages, it's washed with a brine rich in moisture-loving bacteria that renders it "stinky". Though unlike many other washed rinds, the tan-colored exterior stays firm, providing a sturdy boundary for the inner paste to become soft and gooey. The flavors are of freshly baked rolls and buttery leeks, while the rind retains the bulk of the oomph.
Substitutions: Red Cloud (Haystack Mountain Cheese; Colorado, USA), Slyboro (Consider Bardwell Farm; Westboro, Vermont, USA), Cabra Raiano (Casa Lusa; Portugal), Mont St. Francis (Capriole Goat Cheeses; Greenville, Indiana, USA).

CACIOTTA DI CAPRA FOGLIE DI NOCE (C)

Latteria Perenzin (San Pietro di Feletto, Treviso, Italy)

Aged for over three months, this firm, organic goat's milk cheese is wrapped in walnut leaves that impart rich, earthy flavors while protecting the rind. Lemony and bright, the cheese has a distinct tang and a dry texture from those months of aging. Excellent for both nibbling and for shaving (try leftovers on cooked vegetables), this cheese can also be made with sheep's milk—with a different recipe, result and name. Be sure to showcase the beauty of its bone-white paste against the dried, dark leaves.

Substitutions: Robiola di Capra, leaf-wrapped (Luigi Guffanti; Piedmont, Italy), Banon PDO (multiple producers; Alpes-de-Haute-Provence, France), Mothais sur Feuille (multiple producers; Poitou-Charentes, France).

CHEESE LIST:

A Wabash Cannonball

B Cabricharme

C Caciotta di Capra Foglie di Noce

Suggested Accompaniments

TO BUY IN:

kumquats

sweet olive tortas

TO MAKE:

Orange blossom shredded spoon fruit

Large, ripe oranges with thick skins are best for this recipe, and it's a great way to use up oranges after juicing them. The fragrant, slightly bitter zest preserved in sugary syrup goes particularly well with salty white goat's cheese.

6 firm Valencia oranges

1½ cups/300 g granulated/caster sugar

freshly squeezed juice of 1 orange

1 teaspoon orange flower water

1 tablespoon Cointreau or other orange liqueur

1 tablespoon orange blossom honey

sterilized glass jars with airtight lids

heat-resistant thermometer

MAKES 4 CUPS (32 FL OZ.)/950 ML

Peel the orange zest off the oranges into strips using a sharp peeler to make sure no pith is included. Cut the zest into thin matchsticks and set aside.

Bring a pan of water to the boil and drop in the orange matchsticks and simmer for 25 minutes. This will get rid of any bitterness.

Strain the orange strips in a colander and set aside. Return the empty pan to a medium-high heat and add the sugar and orange juice. Bring to the boil, then reduce the heat and simmer for 10 minutes, stirring occasionally, until the sugar has completely dissolved. Add the reserved orange strips and cook for a further 10 minutes.

Remove the orange strips with a slotted spoon, shaking any excess syrup back into the pan and set aside. Add the orange water and Cointreau to the pan and bring the syrup back to the boil. Continue to cook for about 8

minutes until it becomes thick and has reduced slightly. The syrup must read 240°F (115°C) on a thermometer. Remove the pan from the heat, add the reserved orange strips and rest for 5 minutes.

Pack the orange strips and syrup into the glass jars, leaving a ¼-inch/5-mm space at the top. Carefully tap the jars on the counter top to get rid of air pockets. Wipe the jars clean and screw on the lids. The spoon fruit will keep for up to 1 month.

Sheepish

The all-sheep's milk cheese board

Containing more solids—including protein, butterfat and minerals—than goat's or cow's milk, sheep's milk is produced in smaller quantities over a shorter period of time. Since ewes thrive in harsher climates, areas that are not as suitable for cows or larger populations of humans are often left for raising sheep for dairy and meat. Sheep's milk cheeses run the full gamut of styles and should be celebrated for their diversity, depth of flavor and incredible mouthfeel (that butterfat serves an excellent sensory purpose). This board showcases some familiar, excellent sheep's milk cheeses, but there are plenty of others that are not included—including the broad swathe of Italy's fantastic pecorino cheeses (which are all made from ewe's milk; the name derives from pecora, meaning "sheep").

Cheese Descriptions:

ROQUEFORT PDO (A)
Papillon (Auvergne, France)
The blue mold that permeates the paste of this soft, raw sheep's milk cheese was originally cultivated via molded bread. Several traditional producers—like this one—leave bread inside their cave, then, once molded, pulverize and sprinkle it on the cut curd after coagulation. Produced under strict oversight with defining rules about animal breed, location and recipe, Roquefort is a delicate blue with a peppery, lingering bite and a velvety creaminess from the rich sheep's milk.
Substitutions: Bohemian Blue (Hidden Springs Creamery/Hook's Cheese; Westby/Mineral Springs, Wisconsin, USA), Big Woods Blue (Shepherd's Way Farm; Nerstrand, Minnesota, USA), Beenleigh Blue (Ticklemore; Devon, England), Crozier Blue (JL Grubb; Tipperary, Republic of Ireland), Lanark Blue (Errington Cheese; Lanarkshire, Scotland).

MANCHEGO PDO EL TRIGAL (B)
Quesos Corcuera (Castille-La Mancha, Spain)
Made solely from the milk of the Manchega breed of sheep and available in varying ages (3, 6 and 12-plus months), this firm sheep's milk cheese is buttery and deeply flavored. Opt for a more aged Manchego, which develops flavors of ripe olives and hay. The eye-catching criss-cross pattern on the rind is traditional, harkening back to the time when the wheels were molded in woven grass baskets (hence the name "El Trigal", which translates to "wheat field").
Substitutions: Roncal PDO (multiple producers; Navarre, Spain), Pecorino Toscano PDO (multiple producers; Tuscany, Italy), Ossau-Iraty (multiple producers; Pays Basque, France), Dante (Wisconsin Sheep Dairy Cooperative; Bruce, Wisconsin, USA), Lord of the Hundreds (Traditional Sheep Dairy; East Sussex, England), Berkswell (Ram Hall Farm; Coventry, England).

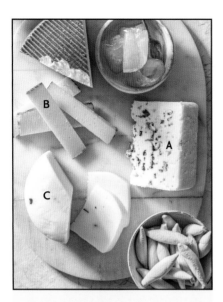

CHEESE LIST:

A Roquefort PDO

B Manchego PDO El Trigal

C Boschetto al Tartufo

BOSCHETTO AL TARTUFO (C)

Il Forteto (Vicchio, Tuscany, Italy)

Although there's a touch of cow's milk added to this wheel, there is no denying the richness and depth of the sheep's milk butterfat here, made even more irresistible by the inclusion of earthy truffle. Il Forteto is a farmer's cooperative that was founded in 1977 with the ideals of inclusion and sharing. Today, the coop resides on 1000 acres and houses a nurturing community for the handicapped; it maintains itself by producing beef, olive oil, pasta, organic vegetables and lots of amazing cheeses available worldwide.

Substitutions: Cacio di Bosco (Il Forteto; Vicchio, Tuscany, Italy), Moliterno al Tartufo (Central Formaggi; Serrenti, Sardinia, Italy), Black Sheep Truffle (Carr Valley Cheese; La Valle, Wisconsin, USA).

Suggested Accompaniments

TO BUY IN:

citrus preserve
mini breadsticks with sea salt
white wine

TO MAKE:

Peppered peach chutney

Summer is the perfect time to make a batch of this delicious yellow chutney. A punch comes from the spices and black peppercorns that impart a wonderfully bold kick to the gentle flavor of the peaches.

12 firm ripe peaches, halved and pitted
4 yellow onions, roughly chopped
5 garlic cloves, finely chopped
2 teaspoons each of ground cumin, ground coriander, chili/chilli powder, whole peppercorns and curry powder
1 teaspoon mustard seeds
2 cinnamon sticks
3 bay leaves
1½ cups/355 ml apple cider vinegar
2¼ cups/450 g turbinado/demerara or sugar
sterilized glass jars with airtight lids

MAKES ABOUT 5 CUPS (40 FL OZ.)/1.2 L

Preheat the oven to 400°F (200°C) Gas 6.

Cut the peaches into 2-inch/5-cm pieces and put in an ovenproof baking dish. Add all the remaining ingredients, apart from the sugar, and toss to combine. Bake in the preheated oven for 40 minutes, stirring halfway through. Add the sugar and stir. Return to the oven for another 55 minutes, checking and stirring every 15 minutes to prevent burning.

Remove from the oven and allow it to sit for 5 minutes, then spoon into the sterilized jars, leaving a ¼-inch/5-mm space at the top. Screw on the lids. Cool, then store in the fridge for 7–10 days before eating. Once open, store in the fridge for up to 3 months.

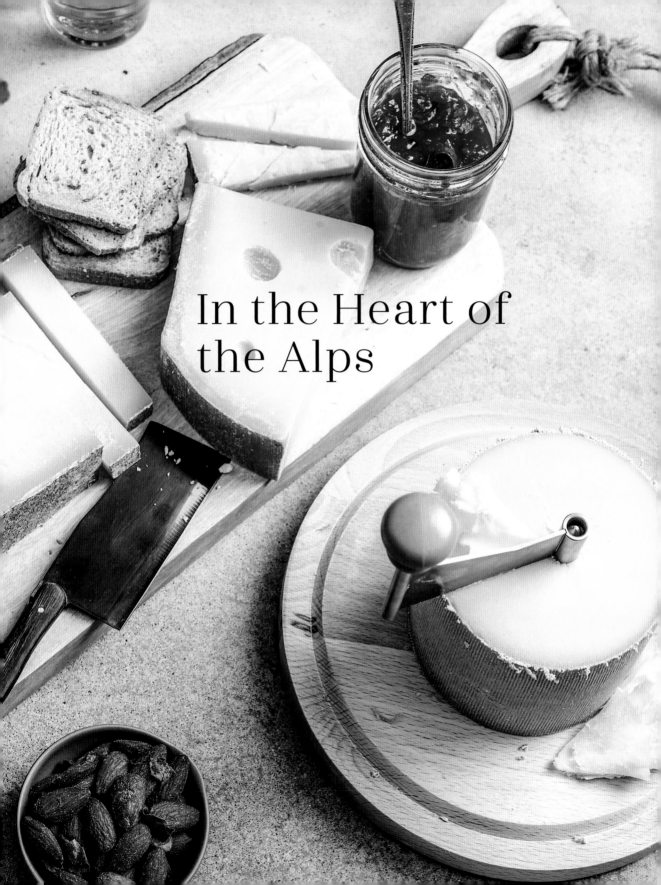

In the Heart of
the Alps

In the Heart of the Alps

All-Swiss cheese board

The magnificent and extensive Alps spread across eight countries, but it is Switzerland that is dominated—both geologically and culturally—by their majestic, snow-capped peaks, lush valleys and wildflower-carpeted mountainsides. Not surprisingly, geography has dictated food production—and traditions have arisen alongside, many of which are central to both internal pride and community gatherings. It is almost impossible to visit the Swiss countryside and not hear the clanging of bells hanging from cow's necks as they munch on pasture grasses. It is the national anthem. If you are able to visit at the end of summer when the milking cows are brought down from the higher elevations (called the désalpe), you will witness the traditions first-hand, and eat more cheese than you considered possible. If you see a cheese labeled "Alpage", that means it is made only from summer milk, when select groups of animals and makers are living high up in the mountains for several months. This all-Swiss cheese board pays homage to the hardworking ladies with udders, the farmers, cheese makers, the affineurs and the land that brings them all together. The term "AOP" means "appellation", and you can read more about this on page 4.

Cheese Descriptions:

LE GRUYÈRE AOP (A)
Fritzenhaus Dairy (Wasen im Emmental, Bern, Switzerland)
This is always made with raw cow's milk and aged for at least five months; its sides are embossed with its logo; its rind is washed with a brine that's shared between all wheels in the aging facility; and it weighs about 80 lb/ 36 kg: this is a much-loved wheel throughout the world, both as a table cheese and in recipes (like fondue). The milking cow's diet changes with the season (though it's only alpine forage, whether fresh or dried) and the aging of the wheels, which is its own profession, ensures that no two cheeses are alike; each is riddled with flavors ranging from herbs and flowers to broth, buttered toast and cooked egg. About half of all production is consumed within Switzerland, but exports still get their fair share. At some stores, you'll find several ages from different aging facilities, which is a good way to educate yourself on how time and care make a difference in cheese making. This particular wheel is aged for 12 months.
Substitutions: L'Etivaz AOP (Switzerland), Beaufort PDO (France), Grand Cru Surchoix (Roth Cheese; Monroe, Wisconsin, USA).

SBRINZ ALPAGE AOP (B)
Alp Chüeneren (Dallenwil, Nidwalden, Switzerland)

Made into 100-lb./45-kg drums and aged for over 18 months (the one pictured is aged for 3 years), this hard, raw cow's milk cheese, like others on this board, has a storied history. While making Sbrinz, cheesemakers cut the curd very small, down to the size of a grain of rice (as with other "grana" cheeses (like Grana Padano and Parmigiano Reggiano). The curd is then both cooked and pressed to expel lots of moisture. Unlike other grana cheeses, though, it is made with unskimmed milk, so the flavors are full, intensely nutty and rich. In Switzerland, Sbrinz is often eaten in thinly shaved rolls that melt on the tongue. It's also commonly served in small chunks, and it grates beautifully.
Substitutions: This is a Swiss original.

EMMENTALER AOP (C)
Käserei Hüpfenboden, "Gottelf" (Langnau, Emmental, Switzerland)

The origin of Emmentaler is indicated in its name: the Emme river valley, near Switzerland's capital of Bern. This iconic, hole-pocked cheese has long been imitated around the world; however, like all food, it will taste of its place—and of its quality. The iconic holes, or "eyes" throughout the cheese's paste, resulting from particular strains of bacteria, are purposefully invited and venerated. Made from raw cow's milk and aged from four to eighteen months, Emmentaler Switzerland AOP has a wide spectrum of textures and flavors but all have that distinctive nutty bite. The Emmentaler pictured is made in the most traditional way and aged for 18 months.
Substitutions: Emmental de Savoie PDO (France), Allgäuer Emmentaler PDO (Germany), Emmentaler (Edelweiss Creamery; Monroe, Wisconsin, USA).

TÊTE DE MOINE AOP (D)
Emmi (Jura, Switzerland)

With a name that literally translates to "monk's head", this cheese has a history that dates back over 800 years to the monastery of Bellelay, in northwestern Switzerland.

Made from raw cow's milk and with a rind washed with a brine, it's semi-firm and strongly flavored, aromatic and best eaten in thin slices. The "girolle", invented in 1982, is perfect for this. It is a wooden round with a central metal piece that holds a thin blade, which scrapes the cheese as it turns, producing ruffle-edged "flowers", see image on the right. Girolles are inexpensive and great to have on hand if you're excited about cheese board presentation.
Substitutions: Raclette du Valais AOP (Valais, Switzerland), Der Scharfe Maxx (Käserei Studer; Thurgau, Switzerland), Schnebelhorn (Käserei Bütschwil; St. Gallen, Switzerland).

TIP: When it comes to cheese, the term "Alpine" is used to describe cheeses made in a particular style that have roots in the European mountains. The most classic example is Gruyère AOP; like other Alpine styles, it has a smooth, cohesive paste, layers of flavors, and is eminently meltable. Alpine-style cheeses are very popular for good reason: they are delicious and (nowadays) made in many places worldwide. Seek them out!

ADDITIONAL SWISS CHEESES

There are many traditional Swiss cheeses, all excellent, that can be added or substituted on this board. A few to try include: Raclette du Valais AOP, L'Etivaz AOP, Appenzeller AOP, Vacherin Fribourgeois, Jura Bergkase, Berner Hobelkäse AOP, Berner Alpkäse, Raclette Suisse, Mutschli, Vacherin Mont d'Or AOP.

PICK YOUR REGION & LEARN BY TASTE

You can make themed regionally-based cheese boards for most countries, regions, U.S. states, etc. Just think about diversity of styles/milks when putting them together and have fun learning while you "travel" to those delicious destinations.

Suggested Accompaniments

TO BUY IN:

rye bread toasts

salted almonds

pickled cornichons/mini gherkins

fresh apricots

TO MAKE:

Tomato & smoked pepper jam

This spicy, smoky jam makes a perfect partner to any cheese board, it is especially good with rich and flavorful Swiss varieties of cheese

4 lbs./1.8 kg tomatoes

2 tablespoons extra virgin olive oil

1 teaspoon sea salt

2 cups/400 g dark brown sugar

1 tablespoon harissa paste

1 tablespoon cracked smoked black peppercorns

1 cinnamon stick

2 tablespoons freshly squeezed lemon juice

sterilized glass jars with airtight lids

MAKES ABOUT 3 CUPS (24 FL OZ.)/710 ML

Preheat the oven to 400°F (200°C) Gas 6.

Spread the tomatoes out evenly on a baking sheet. Drizzle over the olive oil and sprinkle with the salt. Roast in the preheated oven for 40 minutes until the skins have burst and are slightly charred.

Put in a food processor and pulse until coarsely chopped, then tip into a medium-sized pan and add the sugar, harissa, peppercorns and cinnamon stick. Bring to the boil over a medium-high heat, stirring continuously. Reduce the heat to a simmer and cook for 40 minutes, stirring occasionally, until the mixture thickens. Add the lemon juice and cook for a further 5 minutes.

Pour the jam into sterilized jars and screw on the lids. When cool, store in the fridge for up to 1 month.

CHEESE LIST:

A Le Gruyère AOP

B Sbrinz Alpage AOP

C Emmentaler AOP

D Tête de Moine AOP

Coveted References

Books

Cheddar: A Journey to the Heart of America's Most Iconic Cheese by Gordon Edgar (Chelsea Green; 2015)

Cheese & Beer by Janet Fletcher (Andrews McMeel Publishing; 2013)

Cheese and Culture: A History of Cheese and Its Place in Western Civilization by Paul S. Kindstedt (Chelsea Green; 2012)

Fiona Beckett's Cheese Course by Fiona Beckett (Ryland Peters & Small; 2015)

Laura Werlin's Cheese Essentials by Laura Werlin (Stewart, Tabori & Chang; 2007)

Composing the Cheese Plate by Brian Keyser & Leigh Friend (Running Press; 2016)

Mastering Cheese by Max McCalman and David Gibbons (Clarkson Potter Publishers; 2009)

The Art of the Cheese Plate by Tia Keenan (Rizzoli; 2016)

The Book of Cheese by Liz Thorpe (Flatiron Books; 2017)

Websites, magazines and podcasts

Culture: the word on cheese—a general consumer cheese magazine, 6 issues/year. culturecheesemag.com

Cutting the Curd—a Heritage Public Radio podcast series; heritageradionetwork.org

cheesescience.org—an online cheese science toolkit by food scientist Pat Polowsky

Index

Acknowledgements

Firstly, thanks to all the team at Ryland Peters & Small who commissioned and worked to bring this book to fruition, especially Alice Sambrook, Leslie Harrington, Julia Charles and Cindy Richards.

This book would not have come together without the help of Erin Clancy, who helped me to pull together the cheeses for the photo shoot from across the U.S. by calling, emailing and maintaining a proper spreadsheet, and Lydia Clarke, who went above and beyond to ensure that the cheeses for the photos were in great shape. Big thanks to the talented Valerie Aikman-Smith, who took a refrigerator stuffed with the cheeses we sourced and turned them into the boards you see here. Val is the model cheese board maker: she has fun with it, makes sure the cheeses take center stage, and creates her own accompaniments. Thanks also to Erin Kunkel for her beautiful photography.

I owe much to Molly McDonough, who not only fact-checked the manuscript but copy-edited as well (she just can't help it—lucky me!). Former U.S. now UK-based cheese guru Nick Bayne helped immensely with his thoughtful suggestions for cheese substitutions, as did knowledgeable UK-based cheese writer Patrick McGuigan. Erin Harris stepped up to highlight Canadian cheeses when I needed her most and Tony Bogar was, as always, a most dependable and clarifying editor.

Finally, last but not at all least, thanks to the fantastic cheesemakers who rose to the occasion and provided cheese when we were shooting to ensure tight deadlines were met, right at the holidays. It is truly important to have great friends and family. Their support and love ensures success, and I would be nothing without them.